18. APRIL 1974.

KT-539-873

Charles Rennie Mackintosh

Robert Macleod

CHARLES RENNIE MACKINTOSH

Country Life

First published in 1968 for Country Life Books
by The Hamlyn Publishing Group Limited
Hamlyn House · The Centre · Feltham · Middlesex

Copyright © The Hamlyn Publishing Group Limited 1968

Printed in Great Britain by Fletcher & Son Ltd.,
Norwich, and bound by
Richard Clay (The Chaucer Press) Ltd.,
Bungay, Suffolk

Design by Bryan Dunn

CONTENTS

LIST OF ILLUSTRATIONS

PREFACE

There is a good deal about the life of Charles Rennie Mackintosh that is the stuff of legend: his sudden emergence in a provincial city; his colossal output over little more than a decade; his isolation, collapse and flight; finally his death in near poverty and total obscurity. With all this in a *fin de siècle* setting, it is hard to imagine a more improbably romantic basis for a tale.

It would be unfair to say that those few who have written about Mackintosh have added to the sufficiently romantic facts of his life. But in one respect certainly, the popular story has outstripped the reality: that Mackintosh was a lonely genius whose work suddenly emerged out of context, out of time, as a prophecy of the new century. A genius he may well have been, and, at certain key times in certain ways he was a lonely man; but his work, like that of any other mortal, emerged from a real context, and continued throughout his working lifetime to be influenced by that context – and that more in sympathy than in rebellion.

It is this, more than any other single fact, which has motivated and guided this small study; in the background to Mackintosh's work, and in his own references to it, there is sufficient evidence clearly to understand its origins, objectives and perhaps even something of the enigmatic man himself. The limits of this book are therefore narrow. I have not undertaken to survey in it every work of Mackintosh's – even every building project, of which there were not a great many. Nor have I examined the still slightly obscure and tantalising question of the extent and precise nature of his relations with the Continental secessionists – particularly the Viennese. These matters were dealt with in the book that will remain the most comprehensive study of Mackintosh, that by Professor Thomas Howarth. Although certain minor items of fact have emerged since the publication of Howarth's book, it covers those other matters as adequately as need be and it remains the starting point for any

further study. My excuse, therefore, for another study of Mackintosh cannot be that new and necessary biographical data or even technical information is presented here. It lies rather in a complex of facts and convictions, all of which I believe to be important and worth enumerating.

1. The first conviction can be applied generally to the 19th century as well as to Mackintosh and other individual artists. Until recently its treatment by architectural historians has been, for entirely worthy reasons, very largely as a prelude to, and, as the case may be, a contrast with, or a forecast of, 20th-century architecture. While 20th-century architecture may well be more convincing for such a treatment, its predecessors have often been done less than justice.

2. It is a fact that there is a much more clearly defined Victorian ideological progression than has been generally acknowledged, and that Mackintosh stands clearly within it.

3. Curiously, and perhaps significantly, almost the only works known to be by Mackintosh, residing, available to anyone, in the Glasgow University collection, which have yet remained largely without comment or inspection are the draft versions of six lectures in which he attempted to spell out his own intentional framework and his architectural values. The lectures are neither elegant nor original. But in relation to his work and to those influences which he accepted and acknowledged, they are highly informative.

4. The last and remaining conviction – one that began not with pictures or eulogies, but with a first sight of the great grey School of Art hanging over Sauchiehall Street – is that Mackintosh was one of the great architects of British history, not for what he prophesied, nor for what he promised without fulfilling, but for what he was and what he did.

It is a small book, but the obligations I have incurred in its preparation are disproportionately large. I would not have been prepared to undertake the writing were it not for the patient supervision of Sir John Summerson over my more general researches for some years and for the particular stimulus of his short paper 'Some British Contemporaries of Frank Lloyd Wright', which started me off. He cannot, however, be made responsible for the particular views expressed herein. The opportunity to write it would not have taken place but for the encouragement and co-operation of my Director, Professor Patrick Nuttgens. I am indebted to many in Glasgow, in particular to Mr H. Jefferson Barnes, Director of the Glasgow School of Art, Professor Andrew McLaren Young and Mr Dennis Farr of Glasgow University Fine Art Department. These men have been generous with their time and with their knowledge, and they have dealt patiently and promptly with my importunities. Professor McLaren Young has readily shared with me, in a completely unselfish manner, the fruit of his own particular researches and reflections. Similarly, David Walker has been entirely free with his unparalleled knowledge of the Scottish background to the Mackintosh period. If I have produced a wrong balance by not sufficiently emphasising that immediate connection, I trust it will be speedily righted by the publication of Mr Walker's findings. I am grateful to Mr Allen Ure and Mr T. Campbell Lawson for their hospitality. Keith Gibson's craft and care in the photography has ensured that if the book is not read, it will nonetheless be looked at. My wife has ensured that, if it is read, it has a better chance of being understood.

SOURCES

The clear starting point for any study of Mackintosh is *Charles Rennie Mackintosh and the Modern Movement*, by Thomas Howarth (Routledge and Kegan Paul, 1952). This book, with its comprehensive bibliography effectively covers the field of specific literary sources. The one addition to this collection which has been of very great suggestive power, and whose material I have specifically drawn on in Chapter Seven, is 'Some British Contemporaries of Frank Lloyd Wright', by Sir John Summerson, a paper delivered to the International Congress of the History of Art and reprinted *Studies in Western Art*.

There is no adequate study in print of the general architectural scene in Britain around the turn of the century; Professor Pevsner's *Pioneers of the Modern Movement* with its specific interest is not concerned with tracing the entire background to the period, and the numberless progeny of that great work have followed suit without the justification of the archetype. Of contemporary books and periodicals, the rationale and flavour of the 'moderns' of the day can best be found in *The Architect* from about 1889 to 1894, and then in the *Architectural Review* from its inception in 1896 to about 1904.

The lecture notes and diaries of Mackintosh are held in the Glasgow University Fine Art Collections.

CHAPTER ONE BACKGROUND

The architectural scene in Britain in 1890 was full of promise. Throughout Europe the young and the adventurous were watching British developments, emulating British achievements, and imitating British fashions. And, although unknown at that time, there were easily a dozen young architects on the thresholds of their careers who were by their idealism, energy, and gifts capable of bringing that promise into reality.

Yet the promise was never fulfilled. The initiative passed quickly and clearly to the Continent. The most nearly complete survey of the work of that period remains to this day *Das Englische Haus*, the work of a German critic and historian, Hermann Muthesius. It has never, of course, been translated into English. And of the dozen or more young heirs to the promise only one achieved anything like international recognition. That one exception was Charles Rennie Mackintosh, and in the contradiction, enigma, and frustration of his own career are crystallised the turmoil and lost opportunities of a whole generation.

To understand the life and work of Mackintosh, it is first necessary to understand something of the architectural background which he and his contemporaries inherited. It is also necessary to refrain from seeing him as a forerunner of anything until this background is established, for the tendency to identify the architectural intentions of Mackintosh and many of his British contemporaries with those of 20th-century developments, although not entirely without cause, has obscured their stated intentions, and has left many aspects of their executed work quite inexplicable to modern eyes.

In almost every respect the development of architecture in Britain during the 19th century was unique and, characteristically, insular. The reasons were varied. Britain's traditional historic and natural geographic isolation was abetted by her industrial and financial superiority, and what had been, in

other times, a marked sense of cultural inferiority became a startlingly aggressive nationalistic pride. In terms of architecture, it was not nearly as complacent a pride as has sometimes been suggested, and in the latter part of the century there were many voices raised in misgiving over the directions in which architectural developments were moving. But even the sternest critics did not suggest that British architects should look abroad for the solution to their problems; the main, almost the entire, emphasis was on the British condition and on British history.

A great many factors had contributed to this state, but by far the most important of these was the train of ideological development set in motion by Augustus Welby Northmore Pugin. It is now unfortunately assumed that, whenever the name of Pugin is introduced, those of John Ruskin and William Morris will follow in rapid succession, as a kind of Victorian architectural liturgy; but it is not generally appreciated how fundamentally Pugin changed the course of British architecture, entirely apart from the influences of these other very important men. Pugin's great contribution to architectural thought focused on the relationship between architecture and the society which produced it. According to him, the quality of architecture was directly dependent on the quality of the society from which it originated; and the social quality with which he was essentially concerned was morality. Thus his central proposition, that good architecture can only be produced by a good society, gave rise to the infusion of moral attributes to building and the continuing use of such terms as 'truthful expression' and 'honest structure'. In fact, Pugin codified, to a remarkable degree, the doctrine which has subsequently been known as Functionalism.

The fact that Pugin's social message was generated by his fervent Roman Catholicism, and that his architectural message was clothed in an equally intense medievalism, did not limit his influence to the confines of the Gothic Revival. It was because of the enthusiasm for all things Gothic in the mid-19th century, and more particularly because of the enormous influence of the Ecclesiological Society, that Pugin's ideas had such widespread effect.

The Ecclesiological Society began its existence in 1839 as the Cambridge Camden Society, in sympathy with, and in some respects a product of the Oxford Movement. It was concerned with the reform of liturgy and all the artifacts of public worship, including building, within the Church of England. Although an unofficial organisation and the subject of violent attack from both the Evangelical party and the Nonconformist denominations for its sympathy with and emulation of Roman Catholic forms, it achieved through its organ, *The Ecclesiologist*, a widespread influence on the architectural profession. The ecclesiologists frankly and avowedly based their criticisms and recommendations on Pugin's principles; on, for example, his rules that 'there shall be no features about a building which are not necessary for convenience, construction, or propriety', and 'that all ornament should consist of enrichment of the essential construction of the building'. They concurred with his strictures on the imposed symmetry of classical or 'pagan' architecture and with his equal distaste for the equally mannered asymmetry of the Picturesque. They argued together by precept and by example, that the disposition of internal spaces in a building should be demonstrated by its external forms, and that the disposition of doors and windows should be the result of considerations of access, orientation, light and ventilation – not the elements of pictorial composition.

But more fundamentally, the ecclesiologists concurred with Pugin's view of the relationship between architecture and society. And because of the religious views which they very nearly shared, they saw in both the society and the architecture of the

Middle Ages – particularly that of the second half of the 12th century and the first half of the 13th century – a standard which had never subsequently been matched. Accordingly, they proposed that architects must revert to the forms and skills of 'the ancient builders' as a stylistic and technological basis, although they realised that this would take, by the most optimistic estimates, one or two generations, and that until it was accomplished there could be no basis for further exploration or unprecedented invention.

But the facts of Victorian life, in the event, proved too much for even the militant dogmatism of the ecclesiologists. By 1846 they had publicly embraced the doctrine of 'development'. This doctrine meant simply the engrafting of other forms, of foreign details, of modern technology, on to 13th-century English Gothic architecture. What it meant in terms of a new architecture can be seen in Butterfield's All Saints', Margaret Street, of 1849. It is English 13th-century Gothic architecture, built on an impossible urban site, with non-medieval accommodation – such as a Sunday School – with a German Gothic spire, using London stock bricks, and containing exposed cast-iron beams and Georgian sash windows. The result was manifestly High Victorian, scarcely 'Gothic', but – it must be stressed – anything but irresponsible eclecticism.

The influence of the Ecclesiological Society and of its two major architect members, William Butterfield and George Edmund Street, can scarcely be overestimated. For Pugin himself, in spite of his great abilities and immense energy, could never have had anything like the same pervasive influence on Victorian architecture. He was too fanatical in both his religious position and his medieval commitment, too unwilling to adapt to the needs of the society in which he found himself, and, finally, too short-lived. But the ecclesiologists were able to graft his principles on to the stock of the Established Church, subsequently to dilute the archaeological

1, 2 William Butterfield. All Saints' Church, Margaret Street, London. 1849–59. Exterior and interior.

fidelity of the forms in which these principles were clothed, and to adapt them to the requirements and techniques of Victorian society.

This influence was not limited to the field of ecclesiastical architecture, for the Pugin arguments were enlisted in the strenuous dialogue between the 'Gothic' and the 'Classic' camps in the so-called Battle of the Styles. The Goths maintained that theirs was the only style which could be called truly national and indigenous, that it was based on a rational exploitation of building structure and not on an abstract vocabulary of decorative forms, and that (on the principle of development) it was infinitely adaptable to the new and changing demands of modern society. The emphasis was entirely on the national and the rational.

The Classicists found themselves compelled to reply on the same terms, and the result was inevitable. Ultimately both camps found themselves unable to justify strict fidelity to their respective styles on rational grounds, and by 1870 what direct confrontation there had been between the two had effectively disappeared. What remained was the abstracted legacy of Pugin: a compulsion to establish continuity with some native tradition of the past, and to justify that continuity on the grounds of its flexibility and rationality. It is not surprising therefore that there began in about 1870 a revival of the style of 'the brick architecture of Queen Anne and the early Georges', and that this revival was led by men, almost all of whom had begun as convinced Gothicists.

One of these apologists for the Queen Anne was J. J. Stevenson (1831–1908). He argued for the new style clearly on Puginian lines: 'The style in all its forms has the merit of truthfulness; it is the outcome of our common modern wants picturesquely expressed. In its mode of working and details it is the common vernacular style in which the British workman has been apprenticed, with some new life from

Gothic added.' And, to underline the social link and the indigenous basis on which this new style was founded, Stevenson recommended for Scotland the adoption of the Scottish Baronial style. Essentially, all the serious architectural effort that took place for the remainder of the century was founded explicitly or implicitly on these theoretical lines. And although some architects moved towards a more rigid and academic classicism, and some to a more colloquial folk idiom, the final appeal of all was to function and native tradition.

The Pugin influence was not confined to the larger questions of style. Such architects as Butterfield and Street had demonstrated in their work a new methodology of design; an approach that was, as it were, from the inside out, where building forms genuinely were not composed according to either classic order or picturesque imbalance. Indeed, there is often in their work a kind of gauche quality, a deliberate awkwardness that is demonstrably anti-pictorial. It was an approach founded on the tenets of 'truth', 'honesty', and 'reality'. And as the style pendulum swung up through the English Renaissance, it carried with it a growing expertise in free and unprecedented planning and in technological skill.

This technological skill was given great impetus by the contributions of William Morris and the Arts and Crafts movement, for their emphasis on the revival of old skills and techniques, related to the life and enjoyment of the workmen, included, of course, architecture. The Society for the Protection of Ancient Buildings had become, according to W. R. Lethaby, a 'veritable school of building', and under the guidance of Philip Webb had gathered and disseminated a formidable amount of knowledge of building technique and the behaviour of materials. With such men as Webb the inevitable happened, and the question of 'style' became almost irrelevant; if a thing were done well and rationally – responding to climate and site, and using native materials – it would assume a valid style quite naturally and unconsciously. But this was not to say that earlier stylistic idiom must be avoided; a free and wide-ranging eclecticism was positively encouraged, provided the elements were 'assimilated'. Webb, referring to this phenomenon in England's past, described it as '. . . insularising any imported motives. To my seeing there came a sea-change almost instantly on landing, to any fresh fashion adopted from elsewhere'.

It is readily apparent that in this context, where stylistic idiom had become an infinitely variable element, not central to architectural doctrine, in those buildings restricted by size or economy it could virtually be eliminated. And this is what had happened. From the time of the High Victorian Gothic Revival and the parsonages of Butterfield and Street, there had been a continuous tradition of simple domestic building, virtually without decorative embellishment. These buildings must be seen for what they were – from the Butterfield parsonages and the Red House by Webb to the houses of Voysey and Baillie Scott – as one end of a range whose other end often incorporated the most bewildering eclecticism.

This then was the architectural picture in 1890; a loose, free empiricism, at its best refreshingly direct, inventive, and uncluttered, at its worst simply a chaotic pastiche of borrowings from many times and places; but always, at its best, characterised by a relaxed absorption of both past tradition and current possibility. It was a situation which could not have come into being but for the educational and professional circumstances of Victorian Britain.

The British architectural profession unlike its European counterparts, notably the French, had no formal system of education. The customary pattern was an apprenticeship or a period of articles of three years to a practising architect, for which the aspirant

3 James Maclaren. Glenlyon farm-steading,
Fortingall, Perthshire.

4 James Maclaren. Cottages at Fortingall,
Perthshire, 1891–92.

either paid his employer, or at best received little emolument. The system was as good or as bad as the capacity and sense of responsibility of individual employers. There were not a great many places in the country where this informal training could be supplemented by part-time classes. The Architectural Association established in 1862 a 'Voluntary Examination Class' in response to the Royal Institute of British Architects' inauguration of a voluntary examination for architects, but it was not until 1882, when examination became obligatory for Associateship of the Institute, that training began to be systematised. This was still, of course, on the basis of evening classes. The Royal Academy held architectural lectures, and from 1870 had a full-time architectural master, R. Phené Spiers. But it was not until the last decade of the century that architecture began to be recognised in Britain as an academic discipline. While there were undoubted drawbacks in this situation, one of its great merits was that British architecture could never have become bound by academic sterility, or by a single, central platform of patronage. It remained a fluid battleground, where debate and divergence could proliferate, and any able man, no matter how humble his beginnings, could build his platform or win his spoils.

Architectural developments in Scotland during the 19th century, while forming part of the total picture described here, yet retained some national differences. Classicism, in its neo-, romantic, and picturesque forms held a much stronger grip here than in England throughout the century, notably in Edinburgh. This was partly the result of a slightly self-conscious scholastic tradition – Edinburgh's claim to being the 'Athens of the North' – but also undoubtedly due to the irrelevance of post-Pugin Gothic Revival ideology. An architectural appeal founded on a return to pre-Reformation religion and society could not have the same impact in Scotland as in England. Nonetheless, the existence of the strong Gothic Revival contingent in the south did draw from the Scottish Classicists a response in kind, as had happened with their English counterparts. This response could, on occasion, be violent – as in the instance of George Gilbert Scott's executed design for Glasgow University. Among those who objected to this Gothic invasion of the north was the great Glasgow architect, Alexander 'Greek' Thomson. In 1866 he addressed the Glasgow Architectural Society, using the occasion as the opportunity for a three-pronged attack on the Gothic Revival, the unfortunate architect, and the building design. Interestingly, one of his chief grounds of attack was on the 'constructive skill' displayed in medieval building. He acknowledged the skill as indisputable, but as being founded on 'an egregious error. . . . All the parts of Gothic architecture seem to aspire at standing upon end'. Then, widening his field and warming to his task, Thomson went on: 'But perhaps this violent conflict of forces, this incessant struggle between stick and knock-down, may account in some measure for the favour which the style has obtained with a cock-fighting, bull-baiting, pugilistic people like the Anglo-Saxons.'

Such a level of confrontation between Goth and Classicist while highly entertaining, could no more continue in Scotland than in England, and the result was that a common meeting-ground was found ultimately between the two, in the Scottish Baronial style, and the ideological basis of this style, like the Queen Anne in the south, was founded on premises which grew out of the Gothic Revival. The Scottish Baronial prototypes were the latest buildings which could honestly, though perhaps mistakenly, be regarded as completely indigenous, and not foreign importations. They could therefore be used as the basis for 'development' of a true and national contemporary architecture. They also possessed, as did the Queen Anne, evidence of a kind of adaptability, of 'invention', which enabled their chief characteristics to be adapted to various modern functional requirements without violating the essence of the style.

In this self-conscious working out of a national destiny, the same wide-ranging eclecticism became apparent as had emerged from the Queen Anne revival in the south; in some cases it meant merely the addition of a few 'corbie-stepped' gables to the familiar amalgam of Italian Renaissance and 'modern' Gothic details, while in others it meant the thoughtful examination and sympathetic exploitation of national and rational building materials, forms, and methods.

Perhaps the simplest and most direct of such work was that produced by James Maclaren (d. 1890) and by his successors, Robert Watson and William Dunn. Such buildings as the farm-house, steading and 3 cottages at Glenlyon in Perthshire by Maclaren and 4 the inn at Fortingall (1891–92) by Dunn and Watson 5 are earlier than, and fully as deserving of attention as the better known Voysey houses in the south, and stand in the same ideological succession.

This, then, was the bewildering, uncertain, yet curiously promising architectural scene into which in 1889, at the age of twenty-one, came Charles Rennie Mackintosh as a newly qualified architect.

5 William Dunn and Robert Watson. Inn at
Fortingall, Perthshire, 1891–92.

CHAPTER TWO 1863-1893

Charles Rennie Mackintosh was born in Glasgow on June 7th, 1868, the second son in a family of eleven children. His father was a superintendent of police, and the family life in a Glasgow suburb seems to have been normal and uneventful. Charles apparently indicated from an early age a desire to be an architect, and after the normal period of schooling, he was articled, at the age of sixteen, to the firm of John Hutchison in Glasgow.

In this same year, 1884, Mackintosh enrolled as an evening pupil in the Glasgow School of Art. Mention has been made of the relatively primitive state of architectural education in Britain at this period, and that which Mackintosh enjoyed was fairly typical. The philosophy behind it was roughly based on Ruskin's premise that architecture is the art which '. . . so disposes and adorns the edifices raised by man . . . that the sight of them may contribute to his mental health, power, and pleasure'. That architecture was essentially an art of adornment, few questioned; and so it was that the young student spent his days learning the problems and technicalities of raising edifices, and his evenings learning the arts of adornment.

The one atypical aspect of Mackintosh's education was the institution itself, the Glasgow School of Art, and its head, Francis H. Newbery. Since the late 1870s there had been a lively interest in the visual arts in Glasgow, much of it focused on a number of young painters, who, in spite of considerable disparity in their painting techniques and interests, became known as the 'Glasgow School'. Local collectors had been buying important French and Dutch paintings before the work of Millet, Corot, or the Maris brothers had been even recognised in the south, and the influence of all these, together with the Pre-Raphaelites and Whistler, is evident in the Glasgow painters' work. This interest was inevitably reflected in the local Art School, particularly after the appointment in 1885 of Fra Newbery at

the age of thirty-one. Newbery, an Englishman, brought to the school considerable administrative ability, direct knowledge of developments in London, great respect for the work then current in Glasgow, and an even greater respect for creative individuality. Under his direction the Glasgow School of Art became during the 1890s perhaps the finest in Britain, and drew to itself considerable attention from the Continent.

Thus the young Mackintosh stepped into an environment which was not only prepared to accept and encourage the development of individual talent, but which had, demonstratively, already present, all the constituent parts of that artistic phenomenon, Art Nouveau. It is generally acknowledged today, as it was in the time of its flowering, that Art Nouveau owed its prime origin to Britain. But to understand its British manifestation, as well as the enthusiasms and hatreds with which it was laced, it is necessary to understand clearly these particularly British origins.

There were three main constituents in late Victorian artistic ideology which, apart entirely from superficial stylistic influences, prepared the ground for Art Nouveau. The first of these, owing its importance to the obsession of John Ruskin, was the idealisation of Nature. Nature was to the rational the true 'reality'; to the humanist it was the substitute for the Divine; to the artist it was the inspiration for his beginning and the measure of his achievement. The designer, in whatever medium, was sent to Nature to learn of principles of structure, of line and form and mass, of texture, of colour, and of fitness to function.

The second constituent was the emphasis on material and technique, which sprang directly from the Victorian emphasis on labour. It was the doctrine of Carlyle, disseminated by Ruskin, and applied by Morris. Carlyle said: 'For there is a perennial nobleness, and even sacredness in work. . . . Properly thou hast no other knowledge but what thou hast got by nice low effect.

Brick & Stone Arches.
mosaic
W.
mosaic
Red.
Green.
White marble.
White marble.
Parapet.

Modern decoration

Detail of spandril
white ground

import

grey granite

Porfery.

Green
mosaic band.

Green
light red.

S. Eustorgio
Milan

Plan.

6 S. Eustorgio, Milan. From Mackintosh's
Italian Sketchbook. 1891.
Collection : Glasgow School of Art.

working; the rest is yet all a hypothesis of know-ledge.' This general proposition was preached by Ruskin in relation to artistic endeavour, and finally codified by Morris as the very essence of Art: 'That thing which I understand by real art is the expression by man of his pleasure in labour.' This emphasis on the nature of artistic labour led certainly and inevitably to a close preoccupation with techniques and materials, with both the old ways and the new capacities. Particularly in the applied arts, the decorative forms and motifs which were inevitably drawn from nature began to be modified and abstrated more and more in acknowledgement of the methods and media which had brought them into being.

The third constituent of the late Victorian artistic and architectural scene was the changed attitude to history and historical style. It might be termed the principle of absorption. Whereas earlier in the century historical styles had been seen as fancy dress to be assumed with consistency, but arbitrarily, or as the vehicle of an ideological allegiance – as with the Pugin phase of the Gothic Revival – they were seen in late Victorian times as one continuously relevant source-book, where elements from disparate parts of the world and epochs of time might usefully be joined. The underlying conviction was that the conscious and unconscious editing and filtration of the artist's mind would give them a modern relevance and internal consistency.

Thus in the mid-1880s these three ideological constituents were beginning to produce, through their interaction, certain common design characteristics which laid the foundation for a modern style. And it is the prevalence of these ideas which goes a long way towards explaining the otherwise puzzling fact that elements of the 'style modern', or Art Nouveau, began to appear simultaneously among artists who had no mutual contact, and often little mutual sympathy.

One such quarter where a seemingly spontaneous beginning occurred was the Glasgow School of Art, in the work of Mackintosh and his student friend, Herbert MacNair. There is no evidence today of the earliest stages of this stylistic manifestation, but all the common stylistic sources were manifestly present 'in the air' – the craft work of the Morris group, the fashionable interest in the Orient, crystallised in the work of Whistler and his architect friend, E. W. Godwin, and in Scotland a new interest in Celtic art and symbolism. The two young men subscribed clearly to the three ideological tenets, the idea of Nature as the generator of design, the interest in technique, and the principle of stylistic absorption. These attitudes and influences could not in themselves have produced the highly self-conscious style which emerged shortly after 1890 in their graphic and decorative enterprises. The underlying impulse, the incentive, was the compulsion to devise something unmistakably 'modern'. This expressed intention to 'create' a style, no matter how much it might owe directly or indirectly to the past, must be emphasised, for it was to have a critical importance in the later developments in which they became involved.

By and large, there is no hint in Mackintosh's student work, either in architecture or painting, between 1884 and the completion of his articles in 1889, of the precocious individualism which was so soon to set him apart. He did, however, demonstrate marked facility in both directions, and won a number of school prizes for both painting and architectural work. In 1888 and 1889 Mackintosh won national prizes at South Kensington for designs of a chapel and a church; of these schemes only the plan and section of the latter survive, and they are not of great interest. But in the following year, after he had completed his articles and joined the firm of Honeyman and Keppie, he entered for and won the Alexander (Greek) Thomson Travelling Scholarship. Again, the design is not of much

importance. The conditions were of the typical
Beaux Arts variety: '. . . a public hall to accommo-
date 1,000 persons (seated), with suitable committee
rooms, the design to be in the Early Classic style,
and for an isolated site.' Mackintosh's solution is a
competent though entirely typical student exercise in
Beaux Arts planning encased in a slightly uncertain
Scottish variant on Greek Revival vocabulary.

The competition award was of considerable
importance to the young man, for the £60 prize
financed an Italian tour, and it is from this point
that it is possible to follow his ideological development in detail and with certainty.

In February 1891, immediately before his departure for Italy, Mackintosh read a paper to the
Glasgow Architectural Association entitled 'Scottish
Baronial Architecture'. The ideals and architectural
allegiances expressed in it are not reflected in his
student work; hardly surprising, for the world of
student competitions was then treated with a hearty
cynicism, and the nature of designs submitted
generally bore more affinity with the known tastes
of the jurors than with those of the authors. But in
this paper are to be found in embryo all the architectural preferences and intentions which governed
his mature work. The first and clearest of these is,
of course, his choice of subject, a subject '. . . which
has never as far as I remember been more than
incidentally touched on within these walls, a subject
indeed dear to my heart and entwined among my
inmost thoughts and affections . . .' . The introduction becomes yet more fulsome, and perhaps a little
pretentious, but it is the pretentiousness of the maiden
speech, and through the lapsed years it is still possible
to sense the unease of the youth addressing his
elders for the first time. Nonetheless, it is not possible
to dismiss these expressions of 'deep and filial affection' lightly; his life's work has given them in
retrospect a meaning and poignancy beyond the
power of his words. For the work that Mackintosh

produced in his career, by which his reputation was
established, was, within his terms of reference, in
the Scottish Baronial tradition. To understand this,
and ultimately to understand his work, it is necessary to look carefully at his view of the native tradition which he treasured so highly.

'It was . . . the architecture of our own country,
just as much Scotch as we are ourselves – as indigenous to our country as our wild flowers, our family
names, our customs or our political constitution.'
Here, in debt to Pugin and Ruskin, is the foundation
of 'valid' style – its relation to the land and the
society in which it grows. But Mackintosh had
carefully qualified his interpretation of 'indigenous'.
He pointed out that many of the features of the
native style may well have originated elsewhere,
but they had become native by 'absorption'. Thus
he did not deny that many Scottish Baronial features
were of French origin, but argued that they had been
assimilated and modified to suit Scottish materials,
climate, and attitudes; that in many cases they had
probably sprung up virtually simultaneously in
France, England, and Scotland to meet demands
common to all the cultures. Similarly, he argued
that the great Greek and Roman revivals of the 19th
century were irrelevant; that they had been rigor-
ously imposed from without, and that they had
never been 'absorbed' into the native idiom. The
argument owes its origin to Pugin, and is virtually
identical with J. J. Stevenson's plea of exactly
twenty years earlier, for the adoption of the 'Queen
Anne' style in England. At that time, too, Stevenson
had, with remarkable prescience, argued for the
adoption in Scotland of the Scottish Baronial style
on the same grounds. Thus Mackintosh was not
presenting a revolutionary document in any sense.

In his qualitative assessment of the Scottish
Baronial achievement, Mackintosh revealed his personal architectural values in more detail. 'In the
castles of the 15th century . . . every feature was

Quartiere S, Agostino.

Bergamo.

Italian

8 Railway terminus scheme for the
Soane Medallion competition, 1893.
Plans and sections.

SOANE MEDALLION
COMPETITION.

A RAILWAY TERMINUS.
DESIGN BY C.R. MCINTOSH.

useful. In the 16th century also, however exaggerated some of the corbels and other features might be they are still distinguished from the later examples of the 17th century by their genuineness and utility.'
This emphasis on 'genuineness and utility' is marked throughout the essay and is accompanied by a clear belief in the planning of the building being the generator of its architectural form. Thus: '. . . a very marked tendency towards symmetry is gradually creeping in . . . The door is placed as nearly as possible in the centre, and wings or towers are placed so as to balance each other. But there is evidently a difficulty experienced in reconciling the internal arrangements with the external uniformity.

This period of decline although it teaches the architect no artistic lesson directly emphasises the moral that you should not take a plan wholesale and try to fit on an elevation in another style . . .'

But the main lesson of the Scottish Baronial style lay for Mackintosh in its contemporary relevance: '. . . since then (the 17th century) we have had no such thing as a national style, sometimes we have been Greek, sometimes Italian and again Gothic. . . . It is a matter of regret that we don't find any class of buildings but domestic in this style, whether the style can be developed beyond this or not is a point which our forefathers left for us to decide. From some recent buildings which have been erected it is

9 Railway terminus scheme. Elevation.

clearly evident that the style is coming to life again and I only hope that it will not be strangled in its infancy by indiscriminating and unsympathetic people who copy the ancient examples without trying to make it conform to modern requirements.' Almost certainly, it was the work of Maclaren and Dunn and Watson to which Mackintosh was referring, in suggesting that the style was 'coming to life again'. These buildings, with their studied elimination and evocation of the Baronial links with touches of corbelling, or tower forms, and crow-stepped gables are the precise starting-point from which Mackintosh was to develop his own domestic designs.

In February 1891 Mackintosh left Glasgow on his 'grand tour'. He arrived in Naples on April 5th. His diary, which has survived, covers the period from his arrival in Naples, followed by visits to Palermo in Sicily, then Rome, Orvieto, Siena, Florence, Pisa, Pistoia, Bologna, Ravenna, Venice, Padua, Vicenza, Verona, Mantua, Cremona, Brescia, Bergamo, Lake Como, and Milan, to his departure for Pavia on July 7th. His return through northern Europe is not recorded, but on the evidence of the diary together with the mass of drawings produced, the pace he set himself was formidable. He rose each day between 4.30 and 7.30 in the morning, and filled the time with tramping, looking, drawing, and

10 Henry Wilson and T. Phillips Figgis. The Ladbroke Grove Free Library. 1890.

recording. Sundays were – perhaps surprisingly – given over to attending Presbyterian or Anglican church services, if such were available, and writing letters. The cryptic observations of the diary are perhaps a more telling picture of his impressions than the more polished report he gave to the Glasgow Architectural Association on his return, and, brief as they are, provide a fascinating glimpse into a lively, witty, and extremely perceptive mind.

The most striking thing about the diary is the extreme catholicity of taste displayed. There are, however, certain patterns discernible. He showed a greater interest in 'invention' than in academic brilliance; thus enthusiasm for Michelangelo, respect for Palladio; and an inclination to prefer the early work – Romanesque, Gothic, Byzantine – to developed Renaissance building. But the one building which seems to have drawn from him a really negative response was Siena Cathedral: 'To begin with the front is a fraud as it gives no indication of the interior. Then when you examine the design you find that it is almost *not there*. Then you begin to see that were it not for the fine material the whole thing would be very poor as a composition. . . . So much for the front. Then the sides, well they take the cake. There are no windows in the aisles so this part is plain and might look well so, but it wasn't good enough for the Sienese. No they must have windows, so they painted windows along the wall, designed and painted in the Gothic style. Very beautiful (?) examples, and it is a pity that the rain is wearing some parts of them away.' This is the writing of a man who had not only read Pugin and Ruskin, but who had made their architectural premises his own. The architectural concepts of 'truth 'and 'reality' in building were, from the beginning, part of Mackintosh's creed.

His reaction to Siena was not entirely negative, however. He expressed general approval for the campanile and great delight in many details in the cathedral: 'The floor, of inlaid marble, is really magnificent, and makes one sorry that it is a floor. It is partly covered up. . . . There are some fragments of the ancient sgraffito work in the opera which will make your hair stand on end. Figures drawn with shadow only, white or cream or ivory marble ground and shadows a pale and sympathetic green plaster or cement.' Siena received, in fact, perhaps through its initial affront to his architectural sensibilities, far more detailed attention in the diary than any other building. And the attention indicates his perceptiveness, as in his reference to the stalls: 'Then the wooden stalls are really very good, one half late Gothic with just a feeling of Classic about them and the other pure Renaissance. They are undoubtedly good but like most Italian wood-work, they are very stony. Not designed like wood, but stone.'

Mackintosh sent home a selection of his sketches for inclusion in the Annual Exhibition of the School [6] of Art Students' Club, and was awarded first prize. [7] And it was from this event, and these drawings, that his abilities came specifically to the attention of Fra Newbery. From this point on, Newbery's influence as friend and patron had the most important consequences in Mackintosh's life.

On his return from Italy, Mackintosh continued in his employment with Honeyman and Keppie, and with his evening studies at the School of Art. At the same time he embarked on the first of two successive submissions for the Soane Medallion competition. The subject of the 1892 competition was a chapter house. His solution was in an idiom very much in vogue at the time, a sort of free early Italian Renaissance with Byzantine flavouring, the whole articulated within a clearly defined structural frame. The most dissonant element in the scheme is the overtly Picturesque band of false dormers around the parapet, but their extreme linear attenuation gives a hint of the kind of graphic playfulness which was to characterise much of his mature building. Apart from this element, there is a new certainty of handling evident, and a clearly expressed structural discipline. Although unsuccessful in the Soane Medallion competition, this design did obtain for Mackintosh a National Gold Medal at South Kensington later in the year.

The subject of the 1893 Soane Medallion competition was a railway terminus; a subject which demanded a good deal more of the designer in planning and organisation than the previous one had. As with his earlier student schemes, Mackintosh produced a design formally arranged around a series of major and minor axes, formal and monumental, but clothed this time in a variety of what was called 'modern Gothic'. The 'modern Gothic' style was in itself a curious phenomenon of the times; it belonged neither to the rampant eclecticism of the broad stream of current work, nor to the purism of the earlier Gothic Revival. It tended to be used primarily, and not surprisingly, for ecclesiastical work, and two of its chief practitioners were G. F. Bodley (1827–1907) and J. D. Sedding (1837–91). It was based on rather later Gothic models than had been favoured by the Ecclesiologists – late 'perpendicular' Gothic was once more respectable – although it embraced other historical elements on the familiar principle of 'absorption'. But the chief interest of the 'modern Gothic' of the '80s and '90s was the remarkable extent to which a genuinely unified and homogeneous style had emerged. It produced in this period, not only such new devotees as Giles Gilbert Scott and Sir Ninian Comper, but, as a by-product, yet another strand for the fabric that became Art Nouveau.

A hint of this can be seen in the Mackintosh railway terminus project, particularly when compared with some of his later work, for it is easy to see in the flatness and linear attenuation of the great brick surfaces, and the concentration of curvaceous detail around the windows and turret heads, how with little further convolution and abstraction from historic Gothic forms it would become an entirely typical Art Nouveau design. A design from which Mackintosh almost certainly drew inspiration was that by Henry Wilson (a pupil of, and the chief successor to, J. D. Sedding) and T. Phillips Figgis for the Ladbroke Grove Free Library which was published in *The Architect* of June 20th, 1890. Not only does it embody the particular motifs that Mackintosh employed – such as the slender corner turrets – but with its strained symbolism and transitional detailing points, albeit uncertainly, in the direction in which he was to move. A further evidence of this can be seen in a Honeyman and Keppie design of the previous year. This was one of two unsuccessful submissions for the Glasgow Art Galleries competition, and the elevational detail shown was drawn by Mackintosh, although it is doubtful if he was responsible for much beyond this scale; however in the window tracery, and particularly in the patterns of the smaller windows, virtually fully developed Art Nouveau forms are evident, within the 'modern Gothic' framework.

These two Soane Medallion competition schemes are chiefly of value as the only actual evidence surviving of the young architect's professional development prior to 1893. Their stylistic disparity gives little enough indication of his mature work; hints there are, and mannerisms, but the road on which he was to travel was yet far from clear. He had, however, made a small but real student reputation; he was undoubtedly a 'promising young man'. He was employed in a firm which appreciated his abilities, and in which his responsibilities were widening. He was pleasant, gregarious, and articulate. He was passionately involved with his craft, and if obdurate and self-willed, his energy, idealism, and marked abilities made these qualities acceptable to those around him.

8
9

CHAPTER THREE 1893-1896

'It seems to me that to produce any satisfactory work of art we must acquire a complete knowledge of our material and be thoroughly masters of the craft to be employed in its production . . . go to Nature direct for inspiration and guidance. Then we are at once relieved from restrictions of style or period, and can live and work in the present with laws revealing always fresh possibilities.'

The speaker was C. F. A. Voysey, recorded in *The Studio* magazine for September 1893.

The sentiments are readily recognisable, and although at that time his reputation rested chiefly on wallpaper and decorative designs, he had already produced more than one house in what became his typical mode. These houses, with their plain white walls, low-pitched roofs with overhanging eaves, and long horizontal groupings of windows, have often been seized on as obvious precursors of 20th-century architecture. But the fact, as has already been noted, is that they were firmly embedded in the tradition of simple vernacular building that reached back through the parsonages of Butterfield and Street to the social ideology of Pugin. And there were others at this time such as Maclaren and his successors, Dunn and Watson, in Scotland whose designs were equally simple and direct. By the early 1890s there was a clearly emergent fashion for such work, and Voysey, with his undeviating single-mindedness took the lead in this mode. The relative uniqueness of Voysey's position rested on two factors: first, that his architectural output consisted almost, though not quite, entirely of relatively small-scale domestic building in non-urban settings, and second, that his art leaned emphatically on the principle of elimination, rather than 'absorption'. He was greatly, and almost obsessively, insular. This emphasis on elimination produced at its best work that was refreshingly direct and serene, and at its worst, particularly in his two-dimensional designs such as wallpaper, work that bordered on the childish.

The impact of this work, with its emphasis on craft and Nature heightened by its comparatively ruthless simplicity, was considerable, and from its inception in 1893, *The Studio* became the chief vehicle for its dissemination. At the same time *The Studio* had other eggs in its basket, all of which were enthusiastically received by Mackintosh and his fellow students. Mrs Newbery, the wife of the Art School director, recalled forty years later the publication of *The Studio* as the first epoch-making event in Mackintosh's artistic development, and there can be no doubt that the work illustrated in that year, including Aubrey Beardsley's illustrations for Wilde's *Salome*, and a painting by Jan Toorop entitled *The Three Brides*, had a decisive effect.

At about this time – precisely when, it is not possible to say – Newbery noticed in the work of two sisters, day-school pupils, a remarkable similarity to the work of Mackintosh and Herbert MacNair. Thus Margaret and Frances Macdonald were brought to the attention of the two young men, and the four young designers came together for the first time. They were soon christened 'The Four' through the distinction and similarity of their work. Mackintosh and MacNair, who was articled at that time to Honeyman and Keppie, had been developing their graphic interests together. How far they had developed a distinctive manner by this time is not possible to say, but it is certain that the arrival on the scene of the Macdonald sisters, together with the confirmation and incitement of *The Studio*, provided the necessary impetus for the establishment of a fully-fledged style. It is clear that this style, from 1893 onwards, was indebted to the Pre-Raphaelites, to the Japanese, to the Arts and Crafts movement, to Whistler, and to Beardsley; but it was indisputably something quite different from all of these. In essence, it took the products of two schools of thought which regarded themselves as mutually exclusive, and effectively married them.

11 Glass panel. Clear and opaque glass in lead framing. *c.* 1893–96.
University of Glasgow. Mackintosh Collection.

The stream of development which is represented by the Pre-Raphaelites, the Arts and Crafts movement, and, in fact although not in person, Voysey, was built around the idea of the artist's primary responsibility to society. Indeed, that view was so central that it led in the case of William Morris and others to a programme of social reform that quite overwhelmed their artistic activities; but even those who, like Voysey, had no sympathy for the social views of the Morris group, held virtually identical views on the role of artistic activity in society. The arts must embellish, adorn, teach, and elevate society by their form, their content, their manufacture, and their use. The arts must stand for moral uplift, for permanence, for quality. And the inviolable mainspring of the arts was Nature.

The other stream, the so-called Aesthetic movement, embracing Whistler and perforce the 'Japanesque', as the fashion was sometimes referred to, and Beardsley, was founded on the premise that the artist owed duty only to himself and to his art, that he was above and outside the constraints of an essentially philistine society. Similarly, while nature could provide an effective source, Nature was something quite different. It could be much closer to subjective experience than to the perceived world. On this basis the only criteria for assessment were the personal aims of the artist and the qualities of his art. Thus the arts could be – in society's view – immoral, irrelevant, and ephemeral.

Although these views were diametrically opposed, and the philosophical distinction is easily made, it would be foolish to suggest that all the practitioners who were influenced by these leaders made such a clear-cut distinction, and it is equally certain that these young Glasgow designers did not see their activity as bridging the two. But in no other work of the period is there such a balance between the subjective and the objective; between the simple fidelity to material and method of Voysey, and the

12 Poster for *The Scottish Musical Review*. 1896. University of Glasgow. Mackintosh Collection.
13 Repoussé metal plaque: *Gloria in Excelsis Deo. c.* 1893–96. University of Glasgow. Mackintosh Collection.

linear contortion and convolution of Beardsley; between the moral realism of Burne-Jones and the mystic abstraction of Jan Toorop. This is not to suggest that the drawings, decorative panels, and posters produced by 'The Four' from 1893 onwards were in any sense 'great art'. Much of the work was ephemeral in the extreme, much of it was reducible to a simple formula which was repeated with varying success – of rigid rectilinear organisation, with extreme vertical emphasis, attenuated and stylised animal-vegetable forms and colour serving only as muted accents. But it had an inward coherence and consistency which entitles it to the distinction of a 'style' and it provided, in the case of Mackintosh, the basis for later, and more significant development.

It is without question that Mackintosh saw his graphic activities primarily as only one aspect of the larger question of architectural design. He had made this point emphatically himself, in a lecture delivered in February 1893, that is, two months before the first issue of *The Studio*. 'Architecture is the world of art and as it is everything visible and invisible that makes the world, so it is all the arts and crafts and industries that make architecture . . . architecture is the synthesis of the fine arts, the commune of all the crafts.' In fact, this quotation is a direct plagiarism, as are many parts of this lecture, of a book published in the previous year, *Architecture, Mysticism and Myth*, by W. R. Lethaby. What makes the plagiarisms somewhat embarrassing is the fact that they have been invariably the only written statements in Mackintosh's hand on which subsequent historians and apologists have seized to indicate his prophetic thinking. Nonetheless it is important to avoid distraction from the ideological issue, which was that Mackintosh was prepared to subscribe to the ideas and to make them his own. Lethaby's book, his first independent work, was frankly mystifying to most of his friends and contemporaries, yet it was very important in the history

14, 15 The *Glasgow Herald* building. Perspective drawing of 1893–94, and photograph.

16 Queen Margaret's Medical College.
Perspective drawing. 1894.

17 Queen Margaret's Medical College. Plan

of architectural theory. It was probably the first attempt to explore factually the ideological origins of architectural form, to move outside the niggling contemporary preoccupation with localised styles, to explore the metaphysical basis for the phenomenon of 'style'. It is no small indication of Mackintosh's own manner of thinking that he, virtually alone of the architectural profession, should have been so clearly receptive to a work of this kind.

Although he made rather too free use of Lethaby's phraseology – all of the following quotations from the lecture originate from Lethaby – there is no doubt that Mackintosh himself was intensely concerned with the communicative and symbolic power of architecture: 'Of the modes of this (architectural) thought we must . . . distinguish; some were unconscious and instructive, as the desire for symmetry, smoothness, sublimity and the like merely aesthetic qualities, which properly enough belong to true architecture, and others were direct and didactic, speaking by a more or less perfect realisation, or through a code of symbols accompanied by traditions which explained them'.

He went on to generalise about the origins of architectural forms in ancient cultures, and their relation to concepts of the universe; after discussing the role of magic and symbolism in ancient sacred building, he continued (Lethaby again): 'We need not suppose, however, that temples were a sum of these symbols in all cases, if in any; but that from this common book of architecture, each took what he would, little or much, sometimes openly, sometimes with more or less translation, sometimes first hand, often as a half remembered tradition. Old architecture lived because it had a purpose. Modern architecture, to be real, must not be a mere envelope without contents.' Thus while, with Lethaby, he would deplore the use of sham styles, of 'make believe', he did not accept that the gulf between ancient arts and the present was impassable, for the

37

purpose to which he referred was still one of symbolism and of magic – albeit a magic of light, rather than of darkness. 'We must clothe modern ideas with modern dress – adorn our designs with living fancy. We shall have designs by living men for living men – something that expresses fresh realisation of sacred fact – or personal broodings – of skill – of joy in nature in grace – of form and gladness of colour.'

This great plea for modernity – Lethaby's again – has often been quoted on Mackintosh's behalf. But it was one which would have had a widely receptive audience in 1893, and one, moreover, that in Mackintosh's view was already obtaining a wide response among his peers: 'I . . . am glad to think that now there are men such as Norman Shaw, John Bentley, John Belcher, Mr Bodley, Leonard Stokes, and the late John D. Sedding – names most of you will never have heard before but for all that quite as great if not greater artists than the best living painters, men who more and more are freeing themselves from correct antiquarian detail and who go straight to Nature.'

Now, this list of names, even if Mackintosh did not intend it to be definitive, is of great interest. The entire list, with the exception of Belcher, is made up of men who began as 'Gothicists'. In the case of Belcher, the building Mackintosh almost certainly had in mind was his design for the Institute of Chartered Accountants, built in 1889. This building was largely, if not entirely designed by Beresford Pite, who was in Belcher's employ until 1891 and who had begun as a 'modern Goth' himself. And although that building is in a form of 'Baroque' vocabulary, its spirit and organisation is very close indeed to the kind of thing that Sedding and his pupil Henry Wilson were doing with the 'modern Gothic'.

In the work of all of these men the desire to impress with 'living fancy' – to use Mackintosh's (and Lethaby's) phrase – is evident; the desire to create new symbols out of the manipulation and reordering of old forms; to establish continuity with the past, and yet not be bound by it. They were all, to a varying extent, imbued with the legacy of Gothic Revival ideology, and Bodley, Sedding, Bentley, and Stokes could be regarded as being in the direct line of succession from Pugin.

In the light of this, one can understand more clearly the motivation behind Mackintosh's railway terminus scheme, and, more important, one can understand his ideological preparedness for the revelations that the publication of *The Studio* was to bring in two months' time. For in the graphic work of Voysey, and later, in his buildings, could be seen the continuity with past tradition and the reliance on nature made 'modern' in terms of dramatic simplicity, while in Beardsley he saw the basis for decorative exploration which, though using traditional elements, could create a new symbolism.

Although the evidence of these influences became immediately apparent in his graphic work, it is not quite so easy to discover their immediate architectural implications; as a junior in an established professional firm, he could not be expected to revolutionise that firm's output. Nonetheless, over the next two years there are intimations that Mackintosh was able to contribute substantially to some of the office designs – evidence that he was attempting to realise his graphic work architecturally.

At first this evidence appears where one would expect it, as decorative embellishments to otherwise entirely conventional buildings. The first building where this appears to any notable extent is the *Glasgow Herald* building, designed in 1893–94. Here, the organisation of the main block is in an entirely ordinary Queen Anne cum Scottish Baronial cum Victorian commercial idiom. Its only noteworthy elements are the pedimented window heads on the top floor, where the Queen Anne

18 Martyrs' Public School.
Perspective drawing. 1895.

detail has begun to melt and flow under the hot breath of Art Nouveau. But it is in the handling of the tower unit that the mind of Mackintosh becomes clearly evident.

During the Victorian period the office block as a building type emerged, and, with the crowding of cities, economic pressures, and the sharp rise in land values, it became necessary to use awkward corner sites, and to fill those sites completely. As a consequence, the architectural device successfully illustrated here became commonplace. This was to place some multi-faceted vertical element, usually an implied tower form, on the awkward angled corner. The device had the double advantage of enabling the architect to 'turn' the corner and compose the remaining façades independently, and to conveniently place a major entrance at the point which was commercially most desirable, yet architecturally most difficult, the exposed corner. In the case of the *Glasgow Herald* building, the tower image is accentuated by incorporating the water storage and

services at the top. Mackintosh had commented favourably, during his tour, on the Campanile at Siena; he had been much impressed by the dignity of its severe plainness, and by the satisfactory lightening effect created by the gradual increase in the number of openings in the tower as it rose. There can be little doubt that this was very much in his mind as he – and it must have been he – arranged the series of vertical windows in the tower, particularly the top triplet in the plane of the corner extrance, apparent in the perspective although altered in the finished building. But the tower image, almost an illusion, is really maintained by the tall, slender pilasters rising up the angles. Much of their success is due to the small detail of curving them out from the face of the walls, thus implying continuity with the wall planes, rather than articulating them with a sharp angle. This device – repeated in the small top-storey balconies – became commonplace, not only with Mackintosh, but with many of his English contemporaries during this period.

39

The crowning stages of the tower are curious, and, although it is easy to see both their Scottish Baronial and Art Nouveau affinities, must be regarded as a 'living fancy' not yet resolved. The strongly articulated ogee roof, however, has a family resemblance to the railway terminus scheme.

In 1894 the firm designed a small building, Queen Margaret's Medical College, in which Mackintosh's hand is still more evident. According to the record, it was nominally designed by John Keppie, but it is clear that Mackintosh had a considerable part in the scheme, and may well have been ultimately responsible for its basic conception, for the planning of the building is precisely what would be expected from an admirer of 'modern Gothic' rather than from a Beaux Arts-trained designer such as Keppie. The various spaces, disparate in volume and function, are clustered around a central vestibule which rises through the two floors. Each of these functional elements is expressed as a separate form on the exterior, as is the staircase. Further, the disposition of windows is not according to any recognisable system of visual composition, but rather as the precise reflection of the pattern of internal spaces. For instance, the two storeys of windows to the left of the main entrance are arranged in size and location to best serve the rooms within, in accordance with the Gothic Revival principles of 'truth' and 'reality'. Similarly, the tall narrow windows serving the staircase tower decrease successively in height to follow faithfully the climbing treads.

The plainness of the walls, the strongly rectangular quality of the masses emphasised by the use of parapets in conjunction with exposed gables, is very reminiscent, and probably not accidentally so, of the sort of work that Leonard Stokes was doing in England. It is clear that, in precept and practice, Mackintosh was thoroughly in accord with the most progressive English work of the time.

But there was another facet of his architectural interest very much in evidence at this time, his love of inventive graphic detail. Inventive it was, but he insisted on its origin being found in nature. Professor Thomas H. Bryce, the client for this building, recalled Mackintosh peering through his microscope at a segment of a fish's eye, and then drawing the image with great delight. He subsequently returned to the Professor, asking to see more, and confessing that the fish-eye motif had proved decoratively useful in a number of applications. It would be difficult, on this basis, to trace the origin of much of the curious ornament that graced his work, but it can be assumed that all of it, no matter how obscurely, had a natural source.

Another building, displaying similar character, was the Martyrs' Public School, designed about 1895. Here, the disposition of the building's elements is basically symmetrical, a symmetry, however, that is not the result of aesthetic considerations, but of the traditional educational separation of the sexes. Three class-room blocks surround a central hall, and are linked by twin staircases; again, every effort is made to demonstrate this disposition on the exterior of the building. The roof of the staircase, for example, could so easily have been made continuous with that of the adjacent class-room block; instead, it is articulated by means of a thin line of coping running up the roof slope, and by the cantilevered eaves over the large window.

Many of the details of this building are recognisable from the earlier two, such as the vestigial decorative window pediments, and other details which only depart from traditional precedent by the introduction of typical Art Nouveau curves. But there is some fresh departure evident. The cantilevered eaves over the staircase walls are extremely unusual, and forecast a preoccupation that was to characterise all of Mackintosh's subsequent work. This was the creation of novel visual effects by manipulating the physical elements from which the

20 Martyrs' Public School.
Main hall roof trusses.

building was constructed, rather than superimposing extraneous decorative elements. This is even more apparent in the interior, with the treatment of the main hall and staircase roof trusses, and it may well be that the interest in the jointing and assembly of wooden members grew from Mackintosh's increasing involvement during this time with furniture design. It was, of course, in no way unusual for Victorian architects to engage seriously in the design of furniture, although as the century progressed, the days of the 'great patron' receded, and mass-production determined market values, the opportunities for the architect to control the entire visual environment within their buildings rapidly diminished. Indeed, in 1893 Voysey confessed his own ambivalence to his wallpaper designing activities in a way that clearly reveals the architect's interest in, and frustration with, furniture design. He admitted that, were contemporary furnishings acceptable, he would have no use whatever for patterned wallpapers, but: 'as most modern furniture is vulgar and bad in every way, elaborate papers of many colours help to disguise its ugliness'.

Professor Howarth in his definitive study, *Charles Rennie Mackintosh and the Modern Movement*, has suggested that the first emergence of the Glasgow Style, was as early as 1890, in a frieze of cats discernable in a photograph of Mackintosh's bedroom. Although MacNair, towards the end of his life, appears to have identified the room as one which Mackintosh only inhabited until 1891–92, this has always been in doubt, and recent evidence[1] seems to have confirmed a later date – perhaps as late as 1896 when the Mackintosh family was living in Regent

1. Professor McLaren Young has recently acquired an original photograph of the nursery interior designed by Mackintosh for the Davidson family in 1895 for their home, 'Gladsmuir' in Kilmacolm. This shows the identical frieze of cats, and the likelihood is that Mackintosh re-used the stencil in the following year when his own family moved to 27 Regent Square.

Square. Certainly the furniture and artifacts visible in the room indicate a relatively mature Mackintosh style, apart from the graphic certainty of the frieze.

It was from 1894 onwards that Mackintosh engaged actively in furniture design, and in 1895 he rented a small studio where he could carry out various craft and decorative commissions in his spare time. The Macdonald sisters had themselves opened a studio in the previous year, on completion of their training at the Art School, and MacNair, having completed his articles under Honeyman and Keppie, left their employment and set up on his own in 1895. The close collaboration of 'The Four' continued, however, and they became the focus for a considerable number of disciples, well-wishers, and emulators.

During 1894 and 1895 Mackintosh designed several pieces of furniture for the general market, commissioned by the Glasgow firm of cabinet-makers, Guthrie and Wells. These were simple, comparatively severe designs, their rigid rectangularity only relieved by the occasional long, taut, sweeping curve that so characterised his graphic work, and by the 'craftwork' strap hinges and fittings. He avoided the use of varnish, using dark brown or green stains. The result was very close indeed to the quality of the simpler products of the English Arts and Crafts school. The chief difference lay in Mackintosh's tendency to make the structural members slender, often extremely so, with a resulting delicacy and refinement that contrasts with the English homely robustness. This difference, marginal as it may seem, is not without importance. The British precedent for this thin, linear quality, was the immensely popular furniture style initiated by E. W. Godwin, the architect friend of Whistler. It owed its inspiration frankly to Japan, and, unfortunately, the art of the Orient became identified in the Arts and Crafts camp with the Aesthetic movement – at best an irrelevant fad, at worst a dangerous fancy that would seduce men away from true values and the continuing significance of native tradition.

Thus again, as with his graphics, Mackintosh was happily drawing on the merits of opposing attitudes, although it becomes increasingly clear that his beliefs and intentions were far closer to those of the Arts and Crafts movement than they could possibly have realised. And this is essentially the tragedy, for tragedy it was, of the Arts and Crafts Exhibition Society exhibition of 1896.

The reputation of the Glasgow designers, and particularly of 'The Four', was just beginning to trickle beyond the confines of the Glasgow artistic scene, and they were invited to participate in the 1896 exhibition in London. At that time there were two clearly distinguishable attitudes beginning to emerge among the Arts and Crafts heirs of William Morris. One saw its way out of the contemporary stylistic dilemma by a more disciplined and systematic return to native historic precedent than had been characteristic of Morris and his contemporaries. This impulse was underlaid by an increasing self-consciousness both nationally and professionally; nationally, in the desire to explore and exploit the unique qualities of the English Renaissance, and professionally, in the wish to anchor wildly vacillating architectural taste to a standard of historical scholarship. The other group, of which W. R. Lethaby was the principal figure, saw salvation in the literal interpretation of Morris's definition of art as being *anything* done *well*, and thus, architecturally and decoratively, in the abandonment of any pretence to style of any kind. The vacuum thus left was to be filled with concentration on those matters which are loosely grouped under 'function' – on matters quantitative and measurably qualitative. Thus both groups, for different reasons, bitterly opposed anything that purported to establish a new and precedent-free 'style'. This was particularly so of anything that could be identified with the Aesthetic movement

– for the enemy had been clearly defined. William Morris, writing in the 1893 volume of essays produced by the Arts and Crafts Exhibition Society, had observed that there were only two contemporary attitudes to the nature of Art that were really serious, his own – with those of his followers, and that of the 'aesthetes'.

The anger and chagrin of these earnest folk can be understood when they saw what had been invited to their table. Apart from one relatively innocuous hall settle from Mackintosh, the contribution of 'The Four' was largely posters, with some beaten metal work by the Macdonald sisters and one water-colour, rather badly chosen under the circumstances, by Mackintosh. The benign influence of Burne-Jones could not be seen through the malignant presence of Beardsley – and not just Beardsley, for the distortions accorded the human figure in the Glasgow designers' work were beyond Beardsley, and could not conceivably be reconciled with a due respect for Nature.

They were not invited to exhibit again. It did not seem a very important incident. In the south, the Glasgow designers were easily put out of mind; in the north, new and interesting opportunities seemed to be beckoning, indeed some of them as a direct result of that brief southern exposure. For the Macdonald sisters and for MacNair, it was probably a fair exposure; the work shown was representative of their primary interests and output, and their subsequent efforts deviated little from that standard. For Mackintosh, who was before all things an architect, and who was so soon to move on to more meaningful work, it was a disaster, although he may well not have known it at the time. It effectively cut him off from the appreciation and support of those who genuinely shared his roots and values, from the peers whose efforts he already appreciated. It was an exposure too dramatic, too brief, and too soon.

CHAPTER FOUR 1896-1899

The year 1896 brought several important developments for Mackintosh, apart from the London
exhibition. The first and foremost of these was the
limited competition for new premises for the Glasgow School of Art. In 1895 the Governors of the
school were offered a site, a public appeal was
launched, and in February 1896 sufficient capital had
accrued to begin to build. A competition, limited to
eight Glasgow architects, later increased to twelve,
was initiated with a schedule of accommodation
prepared by Newbery. The details of the competition
and its history are more than adequately documented
in Howarth's book; it is sufficient for this study to

note two important aspects of it. First, the amount
of money available for the building was £14,000,
and secondly, Newbery's schedule was extremely
demanding. It proved, in the end, to be too demanding for the budget, and the competition conditions
were amended to bring the two irreconcilables
together; the competitors were asked to design a
two-stage building, with a first stage to be constructed under the specified sum.

The winners were, as history knows, Honeyman
and Keppie. The designer, and he must be admitted
as sole designer, was Mackintosh. It is not as surprising as might at first be thought that a young assistant,

22, 23 Glasgow School of Art. *Below*, the
north elevation, from a modern drawing by
Hugh C. Ferguson. *Right*, floor plans.

PLAN OF SECOND FLOOR

PLAN OF FIRST FLOOR

PLAN OF GROUND FLOOR

PLAN OF BASEMENT FLOOR

PLAN OF SUB-BASEMENT FLOOR

still a considerable distance from partnership, should have been entrusted with this design. Honeyman and Keppie were an established firm, with a considerable amount of work, and the project was in no way an enviable one. It was not a building to which a great deal of prestige could be attached, and it was, in financial terms, both a small job and a relatively demanding one. But the second reason may well have been the overriding one. The reins of power in this competition were ultimately in the hands of Francis Newbery. And Newbery was not just Mackintosh's former teacher; he was his friend, patron, and admirer. The furore that followed

24 Glasgow School of Art.
The north façade. 1896–99.

the publication of the winning drawings, unmistakably in Mackintosh's hand, was to be expected. In retrospect, it did not amount to much, and centred primarily around the 'modern' details. These details in themselves did not amount to much; they are no more than had appeared in earlier productions by Honeyman and Keppie.

The design itself, as submitted in October 1896, is of compelling interest and great importance, for it heralds the arrival of a major architectural talent, and initiated a building which bears in its fabrics the trace of that talent's development over the following thirteen years. It must be emphasised that the design itself was in no way a fixed and final thing; to Mackintosh it indicated an intention, and that intention remained in flux, subject to refinement and improvement as the building details emerged until the physical completion of the fabric.

But what of the first design, of the intention? Initially it was the site that determined the character of the scheme. This was a long narrow rectangle lying east to west on the south side of the principal access street. There was a tremendous slope from this access street down to the southern boundary of the site, which was abutted by a heterogeneous mixture of buildings. The east and west boundaries gave on to secondary streets.

A school of art consists basically of a series of studios connected by corridors and served by various offices, cloakrooms, class-rooms and attendant spaces. Studios require north light, and the light they get must be relatively constant, disrupted neither by sun nor shadow. Large windows would be needed for studios of the size that Newbery specified.

It is immediately apparent that on this site the studios would have to be placed on the north, that is the entrance, face. The depth of the site was such that the major spaces, other than studios, could not be accommodated in the remainder, allowing for the width of a reasonable access corridor to the studios.

48

25 Norman Shaw. New Zealand Chambers, Leadenhall Street, London.
26 *Opposite*. Glasgow School of Art. The entrance bay.

The result was a plan in the shape of a stubby letter 'E', with a symmetrically placed entrance and staircase, the ends terminating with elements such as the library and lecture rooms, to the south of the studios.

It was, in fact, a simple, logical plan, whose sensible determination was in a virtually complete axial symmetry. And it is here that Mackintosh betrays his British, and uniquely British, antecedents and affections, for the building is almost perversely asymmetrical. It is, further, an asymmetry that cannot be justified pictorially, for the difference in the sizes of the great studio windows, while being readily perceptible on the ground, are not sufficient to create any sense of visual drama, or even progression. They are simply, and under the circumstances, almost fanatically, reflective of the varying sizes of the studios within. There can be no doubt whatever that Mackintosh was not only aware of, but committed to the Gothic Revival principles of design referred to earlier. It would have been the simplest of mathematical exercises to have produced a window size and proportion which would have served the slightly varying sizes of studio, and yet have produced a uniform exterior bay spacing. This is not to suggest that he was at fault; indeed, the whole school of thought which had led to this decision was the most pregnant with hope in the architectural scene. Mackintosh's commitment to it was in no small way a tribute to his perception, and it contributed, in turn, to his greatness.

The same attitude of mind is evident in the treatment of the entrance bay. Here again, the asymmetry is justified by the logical disposition of the spaces behind. The asymmetrical balance is, of course, much more carefully considered pictorially, as might be expected in view of its prominence, and the fact that it is a single element whose internal visual coherence must be maintained. There was, of course, a good British precedent for this calculated imbalance. Twenty-four years before, Norman

27, 28 Glasgow School of Art.
The east façade and detail.
29 *Opposite*. Detail of railings on
the north façade.

Shaw, whose work Mackintosh so much admired, had built the revolutionary New Zealand Chambers in London. It heralded the arrival of the so-called Queen Anne movement in the commercial centre of the city. Comparison between this building and the Art School reveals remarkable similarities of handling, not only in the carefully contrived relationship between the off-set door and small oriel window, but also in the larger relationship between the solid entrance bay and the big multi-paned windows on either side.

The visual game that Mackintosh was playing is heightened by the bay spacing of the very prominent front railings. These are precisely symmetrical on either side of the front entrance, indicating, among other things, that the entrance door is in fact in the physical middle of the building. Not only that, but each of the piers, as can be seen in the elevation drawing, arrives at some immediately identifiable relationship with the window spacing behind, with one exception. Thus the determination to let function govern the disposition of the basic elements detracted in no way from attention to visual detail. The actual form of these railings is of interest, for they can be directly related to a building designed a year earlier, the Passmore Edwards Settlement, now the Mary Ward Settlement, by Dunbar Smith and Cecil Brewer. In this building there is a similar feeling in the semicircular arch over the principal entrance, and in the thin horizontals of the canopies.

Mention has been made of the way in which the design of the Art School, as with all of Mackintosh's later work, was changed and modified as the scheme and the building developed. This was in itself an ideological principle, and characterised most of the work of men who owed allegiance to the teachings of Ruskin and Morris. It owed its origin to the idealised view of medieval society; of a relationship between intelligent craftsmen, each of whom contributed creative skills within an intentional frame-

30 Dunbar Smith and Cecil Brewer.
The Mary Ward Settlement, Tavistock Place,
London. 1895.
31 *Opposite*. Glasgow School of Art.
Brackets to studio windows.

work provided by the Master Builder. Faced with the facts of Victorian life, however, the process became subtly modified. Craftsmen, even if skilled, were given neither ·the facility nor the economic opportunity to be creative, and so a process evolved where the architect himself, on occasion with the participation of superior sculptors or mural painters, engaged in a developing dialogue with the tradesmen on the site, altering and refining details as the concept emerged into a reality. It was, and is, a process which, while giving a great deal of opportunity for second thoughts and refinement as building problems emerge, tends to make the reconciliation between the initial estimate for a building and the final account an impossible exercise.

The changes that occurred in the building of the first section of the school were not major, but taken together they indicate a thoughtful reassessment of every detail of the building fabric. The turret form enclosing the private staircase from the Director's office to his studio was modified and more strongly articulated; small windows were added here and there, and the railings and other ironwork were changed. The entrance door and surround were given a more Art Nouveau form, and the gate pillars received a shallow ironwork arch. One apparent change which is, however, illusory, was the cantilevered roof over the great studio windows. The element which appears on the first elevation as a shallow dentil cornice is in fact this cantilevered roof

32, 33 Glasgow School of Art.
The main staircase rising to the first floor
level, and from ground level.
34, 35 *Opposite*. Roof trusses supporting
Museum roof light, and Museum.

and its wooden brackets in dead elevation. The low
parapet wall shown above this roof line does exist,
although it is invisible from the street.

The projecting iron brackets to the studio windows
have never escaped attention in any commentary on
this building and whatever attributes critics in
their wisdom have given them, they do display one
overriding characteristic of Mackintosh's mature
decorative enterprise. They are, in the definition by
Fergusson with which every Victorian architect was
familiar, 'decorated construction' and not 'constructed
decoration'. They are used to support window
cleaners' planks – an entirely necessary provision,
and they provide some bracing to the window
mullions. With this functional justification, they became the inevitable subjects for Mackintosh's graphic
whimsy, and thus the most discussed window
brackets in history.

The main staircase and first floor museum taken
together form a fascinating catalogue in timber of
Mackintosh's influences and predilections: the modern
medievalism of the heavy trusses with their lovingly-
expressed tenoned and dowelled joints, the stressed
Voysey quality of the balusters and newel posts,
and the Japanese twinned beams projecting and
gripping the newels. Withal, it possesses a remarkable
unity, and presages a developing preoccupation with
space and its manipulation.

Another more prosaic but equally revealing aspect
of the building deserves attention. It incorporated a
fully integrated, and by all reports most effective,
plenum system of heating and ventilation. Under the
central corridors at sub-basement level runs a warm-
air duct. It is, for most of its length, some six feet
high and the full width of the corridors above, and
was served by a large fan-room adjacent to the boiler
room. Large fresh air grilles were located beside and
below the main entrance, and the main duct fed
vertical branches built into the corridor walls which
in turn opened into the studios through grilles. The

36 Glasgow School of Art. Detail of
air duct in sub-basement.

system was extremely carefully considered in relation
to the building design; its abandonment some years
ago and the substitution of the usual unconsidered
jungle of pipes is inexplicable. The system as originally installed was not revolutionary for its time, con-
trary to some belief; but it did require a high degree
of integration with the architectural layout in early
stages of planning. And its final complete unob-
trusiveness in the building speaks highly of the
architect's concern for the environment, and not
just the visual picture he was creating.

Of the rooms finished in the 1897–99 phase of the
Art School building two in particular indicate the
direction in which Mackintosh's style was moving.
The room originally used as a Board Room, in the
east wing, is an airy, simple space, beautifully lit
by two tall windows in each of the east and west
walls. The quality of the light is consciously enhanced
by pushing the windows out into bays and providing
white painted, curving 'cheeks' as reflective surfaces.
The large steel beams spanning the ceiling are
exposed and painted white, doubtless an economy
measure, but one which was clearly happily accepted,
and their position clearly determines the location
and size of the elegant fireplace surround. Even more
indicative of certain development is the Director's
office. It is another white room, with painted panelling. But here the panelling is carried uniformly
around the room, tying together door heads, fireplace surround, cupboard doors, staircase opening,
and window rail. It sharply delineates the wall from
what is to be read as the ceiling. In this room, as in
most of his future rooms, the ceiling is modelled
in such a way as to emphasise the function of certain
areas. For instance the recess into the window bay,
clearly a writing or study space, is marked by a
shallow arch at a considerably lower level than the
general ceiling. It springs, in fact, from the top of
the dado, and creates a significant change in scale
within the total space. In this room two different

37 The original Board Room in the east wing, now the Mackintosh room.

38 Glasgow School of Art.
The Director's Room.

levels of design interest are fused together – levels which all too frequently remain dissociated. The first is the interest which locates a room and determines its principal elements such as windows and doors, the second, that which then analyses the disparate activities that take place within that room providing for them by means of fittings and furnishings. What is beginning to be apparent here, and was to become even more marked, is their interaction; for instance the small-scale consideration that provided a suitable size and situation for the writing recess early enough in the design process for it to appear as an exterior element on the face of the building.

The opportunity to explore problems of interior design on a large scale came in the year of the Art School competition, with Mackintosh's introduction to Miss Catherine Cranston. Miss Cranston was one of that special breed of women who rise to prominence in every generation, combining a shrewd and precise business acumen with an equally precise taste and flair for the dramatic. With her father's help, and subsequently that of her husband, she established herself in the tea-room business. This was a particularly Glaswegian phenomenon of the turn of the century, an enthusiasm for non-alcoholic places of refreshment that combined the facilities of gentlemen's midday clubs with the gentilities of ladies' afternoon tea. In a remarkably short space of time Glasgow became served with a very high standard of public catering. When Mackintosh met Miss Cranston, she was firmly established, but merely on the threshold of a remarkable programme of expansion.

At the time of their meeting, Miss Cranston had two premises undergoing structural and decorative preparation for catering, in Buchanan Street and Argyle Street. Over the following two years Mackintosh executed work for both of these, in conjunction with other designers, notably George Walton.

These establishments were rather more extensive than is suggested by the name. They included tea-rooms, luncheon-rooms for each sex, general luncheon-rooms, dinner-rooms, billiard-rooms, and smoking-rooms. They provided the designers with opportunities for whimsy and decorative extravagance not normally acceptable in ordinary architectural commissions.

It is not therefore surprising that in the Buchanan Street premises, to which Mackintosh contributed only murals in association with Walton's furniture, he simply transcribed his highly effective poster technique in terms of bold stencilled patterns. But even with these highly personalised forms, his allegiance to Arts and Crafts principles is evident. Voysey, in the interview recorded in the first issue of *The Studio*, had emphasised the necessity to show the ties in stencilled patterns – in other words, the technique must be clearly evident as 'honest' design, and there must be no attempt to create the illusion of conventional painting. It is evident that Mackintosh consciously adhered to this – the pattern of the ties is not only apparent but is organised to provide an additional rhythm in the design.

In the following project, the Argyle Street Tea-Rooms, Mackintosh's contribution was again a limited one, this time to the movable furniture. In this furniture many typical Mackintosh forms can be seen emerging. Like his work in other fields, it shows the curious blending of Arts and Crafts traditional forms with the severely linear qualities of the Godwin-Aesthetic school. But there can be seen too his sometimes quixotic delight in pursuing functional considerations to inventive ends. The buttock-shaped recesses in the wooden stool surfaces would certainly require a posterior commitment of unreasonable accuracy.

These two small projects laid the foundation for a continuing collaboration which was to extend over twenty years, and was to provide Mackintosh with

42, 43 Queen's Cross Church, Glasgow. 1897–99. Exterior views.
44 *Opposite*. Queen's Cross Church. A side aisle.

one of the most important of the tragically small range of opportunities that came his way.

During the time that he was engaged on these first tea-room projects, Mackintosh was, of course, fully occupied in the office. He began work on a design for a church at Queen's Cross, Glasgow, immediately after finishing the Art School competition drawings. This was a project of considerable importance, not only for its own intrinsic interest, but as a revealing indication of his allegiance to tradition. For a church presented no startlingly new functional demands, although its forms and fabric were steeped in meaningful symbolism and association; this was no less true, although in certain symbolic respects more negatively true, for the Church of Scotland than for the Church of England.

The most notable characteristic of this church,

then, is its traditional handling. This is not to say that it was not, in contemporary terms, modern, but it is the modernity of those who placed a high value on past ways, the modernity of Bodley, of Bentley, Sedding, and Stokes. Howarth's discovery of the source for the tower and engaged turret in a sketch of Merriot Church, Somerset, is of interest in this regard, but it is also worth noting how Mackintosh justified, or at least excused, the use of the particular form by the internal planning of the gallery staircase. Of course, in its details the church became the subject of Mackintosh's personal inventiveness; but even here, it was little further removed from historical precedent than, say, Stokes' Church of St Clare at Sefton Park, Liverpool, of 1888–90; in both there is a clear dependence on the precedent of Bodley and Sedding. It is worth noting, too, how

Opposite

Windyhill house, Kilmacolm. 1899–1901.
The north façade.
Project for the Music Room. Reproduced
from *Haus eines Kunstfreundes* published
n Darmstadt by Alexander Koch in 1902.

45 Queen's Cross Church.
General view of the interior.

essentially close the handling is with the east end of
he School of Art, even to the predilection with
he engaged octagonal form. Of course the Art
School was plainer, but this was the product of
propriety and economy, not of 'modernity'. The interior details of the church give a true picture of what
was meant then by 'modernity'. The great steel roof
ies, frankly exposed with their pattern of rivets,

owe little to tradition – but they are in the same
place as, and fulfil the same role as the great adzed
timbers of a medieval roof. And every other element, 44
even to the 'east' window, although answering 46
tradition, is, on inspection, novel both in form and 47
detail. Certain of the details here, notably the gallery
balustrading with its posts and pendants, recur time
and again, with variations, through Mackintosh's

later designs – as in the interior details for the *Haus eines Kunstfreundes*, the Oak Room for Miss Cranston, and finally in the library of the School of Art.

One other point is deserving of notice here. Critics past and present of the graphic innovations of the Macdonald sisters, MacNair, and Mackintosh have accused them of a conscious wish to outrage, and even of possessing a tinge of moral decadence. There can be no doubt that much of this feeling can be directly attributed to its association in the minds of the critics with the whole Oscar Wilde–Aubrey Beardsley ethos; it is perfectly clear that 'The Four' saw no such sinister symbolism in their own work. They were developing what they felt to be a meaningful iconography for a new age out of the forms of the past, and Mackintosh could use these writhing, curiously organic forms for the tracery of a church window with a sense of perfect propriety.

This attitude was realised with some surprise by Gleeson White, the editor of *The Studio*, in 1897. His was the only voice publicly raised in support of the Glasgow designers during the Arts and Crafts Exhibition of 1896, and he subsequently visited the group to investigate their work further. The result was a pair of articles in *The Studio* during 1897, entitled 'Some Glasgow Designers and their Work'. Not only was White astonished at the youth and 'wholesomeness' of the designers, but at the absence of a revolutionary attitude. Of the Macdonald sisters he said: 'With a delightfully innocent air these two sisters disclaim any attempt to set precedent at defiance . . .'. What White did not perhaps realise was that the sisters retained through their lives serious religious convictions, and they were quite as prepared to use their art to depict the Annunciation and the Nativity as Beardsley was to illustrate the *Lysistrata* of Aristophanes.

These articles by Gleeson White were the only

significant benefits accrued by the 1896 London exhibition. *The Studio* was avidly read on the Continent, and as a result Alexander Koch of Darmstadt published an article on the Glasgow designers in *Dekorative Kunst*, in November 1898. Thus began an appreciation that was to sustain the designers and stimulate them through many years of apathy at home.

In 1898 a competition was held for the design of an International Exhibition to be held in Glasgow in 1901. Honeyman and Keppie submitted three 48 schemes, one of which was by Mackintosh. Although unsuccessful in the competition, his design is of interest in showing his developing style applied to a new problem. Whilst relatively conventional in plan and even in the disposition of the elements, 50 the forms used are probably more radical than any he used in his architecture before or since. It is entirely likely that the temporary nature of exhibition building made Mackintosh feel justified in abandon-

ing his reliance on 'tradition' to an unusual degree – it was not, perhaps, entirely 'serious' building. The quality generated, however, is extremely gay and appropriate, and there is a certainty and verve about the handling that makes this work, among those who were attempting to be 'modern', astonishingly unusual. This quality is particularly apparent in the design of the Concert Hall, although knowing Mackintosh's immense capacity for re-orienting and transforming borrowings, it may well owe something of its form, and the forms of the butt-resses, to the roof domes then being constructed on Bentley's Westminster Cathedral.

In the meantime, 'The Four' disbanded. Herbert MacNair accepted a post as Instructor in Decorative Design at Liverpool University in 1898, and the following year married Frances Macdonald. Their departure cannot be considered in any sense a handi-cap to Mackintosh's development, for although he and MacNair were close friends, there was no doubt

50 Project for an industrial hall, 1898. University of Glasgow. Mackintosh Collection.
51 *Opposite.* Windyhill. The north façade. 1899–1901.

as to who was the prime mover in the artistic relationship. MacNair never undertook any architectural work, and his subsequent decorative efforts did not move significantly beyond his youthful Glasgow level. The difference between the men was noted by Augustus John, who was a contemporary of Mac-Nair's at Liverpool, and subsequently friendly with Mackintosh in Chelsea. For MacNair he had little but scorn, for Mackintosh a considerable respect, even in his decline.

As the century drew to an end, and Mackintosh moved into his thirties, the prospect was fair. He had a position of some seniority in the firm, and was being given a free hand with some interesting building projects. His private practice was beginning to develop, and the decorative commissions he had executed received publicity disproportionate to their size. Life was very full, and though the demands were beginning to be heavy, his energy and enthusiasm were equal to the challenge. He had always been intense and determined; but the intensity, in these happy circumstances, could find expression in high enthusiasm, and the determination was couched in a very real personal charm.

CHAPTER FIVE 1899-1901

The development of the detached family house during the latter 19th century was the one area of architectural effort above all others in which British architects were universally deemed to have excelled. This was so much so, that the interest in British domestic architecture, both at home and abroad, became almost obsessional. From the 1890s to the outbreak of the First World War domestic and foreign journals were filled with plans and cloying little perspectives; competitions for designs for non-existent clients on non-existent sites were organised, and, almost obscured by the honey-suckle and the thatch, a considerable body of meritorious work was actually achieved. Riding the crest of this wave of popularity, and no doubt slightly bewildered by it, was C. F. A. Voysey. With its sheer innocent directness, his work created an imagery which, almost by accident, won the affection of an age sated with eclectic excess. Similarly popular, and for similar reasons, were the quaint domestic exercises of Hugh Mackay Baillie Scott; although his houses, with their adzed beams, cosy ingles, and childlike stencilled patterns had little of the cool clarity of Voysey, the appeal to

traditional values and the self-conscious informality of both were much the same.

In 1899 Mackintosh received his first independent commission for a house (excluding an unimportant pair of houses built for his uncle in 1890). The client was William Davidson, for whom he had already carried out some minor decorative work. Davidson was a discerning patron of the arts, and an admirer of Mackintosh's work. The architect thus found himself in an ideal situation for exploring and exploiting his convictions with the full sympathy of his client.

The site is located high on a south-sloping hillside on the outskirts of the town of Kilmacolm. It has a panoramic view of rolling, pastoral landscape, and is served by a road running along the northern border. The house is set on a slight plateau somewhat below the level of the road and separated from it by a small courtyard; from the south front the garden swings away down a steep slope of terraced planting to an enclosing garden wall below.

The appearance of Windyhill is curiously paradoxical; it combines the traditional and the unprecedented, the casual and the precise, the bleak and the picturesque. The materials and their constructional assembly are all entirely traditional, conforming with considerable technical awareness to the best accepted practice. The structure is of whin stone finished with brick around windows and doors for easy working; the whole including the returns around door and window openings is then rough-cast – the economical and effective ancient Scottish response to rains that fall horizontally as often as vertically. In accordance with the same precedent, the walls rise beyond and protect the gable ends of the roofs, which are finished with slate.

As one would expect by now, the insistence that elements be disposed by function and not by appearance is quite evident, but at Windyhill there is an

FIRST FLOOR

GROUND FLOOR

odd compulsiveness about it, as when the roof guttering is allowed to bisect the dormer windows on the north face, when windows are not only misaligned in position and size, but their very panes vary from one to the next. This in itself is not unusual; it is an expression of the conscious gaucheness, the anti-pretty attitude that had as its chief historical exponents William Butterfield and Philip Webb. What *is* unusual is that together with this can be seen Mackintosh the post-traditionalist, the formal graphic composer at work, as in the artful lapping planes of the entrance porch element and the stair tower, the thin, flat planes of the nursery alcove and the south bay window. The appearance of irresolution is further heightened by the self-consciously artful garden wall. This, with its rubble texture, patches of dressed coping, its curves and swoops along the boundaries, even its casual embrace of an ancient bothy, is a country dance by a ballerina, a faintly uncomfortable parody.

But what of the plan that generates such ambivalence? It is clear, direct, and eminently workable. Indeed, it is so clear as to suggest a much simpler external resolution than emerged. Again, as might be expected, it is characterised not only by the thoughtful functional relationship of rooms one to the other, but that consideration of the precise proportions, of the placing of doors, windows, and fireplaces, that betrays Mackintosh's microscopic concern with details of living. This concern, finally expressed by the carefully detailed built-in fittings, and such whimsically attractive elements as the window alcove in the upper-floor corridor, produces a sense of resolution that is as marked internally as it is absent without. It is, by any standard, a notable house. In the context of Mackintosh's development it is brimming with possibilities, a clear indication of the direction in which he was to move.

There are two small designs dating from 1901, the year in which construction of Windyhill was

completed, which almost suggest that Mackintosh was exploring in the abstract the problems raised by Windyhill. A town house and a country cottage 'for the artist' were the subjects, and they form a related pair. While they are only sketch designs, with no indication of construction or detail, they are manifestly intended to be read as being of much the same combination of materials as found at Windyhill. The plans are simple in the extreme, and, while adequate, are essentially of interest only in the way they determine the exterior of the buildings. These are exterior studies, exercises in pictorial architecture. Although the plans still determine the exterior, and, as far as can be determined, the rooms are properly served by their windows, the elevations are carefully and precisely controlled. The accomplished graphic artist is now very much in evidence, and if the elevations owe something to Voysey, and in turn to the artful imbalance of Norman Shaw, they are nonetheless original and highly personal. They do contain affectations, however, that characterise none of his executed work, for instance the wilful line of the parapet in the country cottage, that pays scant heed to the actual roof line, and would have been not only expensive to build, but technically irresponsible. But the importance of these little exercises is that they show the transfer of his graphic skill to an area not yet mastered.

In the same year, Mackintosh produced another design which, although also unexecuted, demonstrated far more dramatically his growing architectural certainty. The *Zeitschrift für Innendekoration* sponsored an international competition for the design of an Art Lover's House. Mackintosh's entry received that distinguished prize of so many worthy competition entries, second place, the place beloved by architectural cynics as receiving much of the glory, some of the profit, and none of the grief of the winner.

The winning scheme was by Baillie Scott, a design

55 *A Country Cottage for an Artist*. 1901.
Elevations and plans. University of Glasgow.
Mackintosh Collection.

56 *Haus eines Kunstfreundes.*
Perspective drawing. 1901.

THE ·GLASGOW·
SCHOOL·F·ART·
LIBRARY·

that disported itself quaintly around an axial symmetry in ranks of conical turrets, rounded gables, chimney-stacks, and calculated inconsistencies. It combined all that was implausible about the Arts and Crafts image, and with its institutionalised medieval fantasy lost both the practical sense and the simple directness of that movement.

The Mackintosh scheme stands out in startling contrast. Its roots, to be sure, are in traditional building methods, but once this is acknowledged it can be forgotten, for the way in which these traditional materials are used generates a quality which is quite new. The intimation of the forms used was evident in Windyhill, and they were obviously explored in the two small designs, but what was irresolute in the executed building and was in danger of degenerating into too-pretty whimsy in the small schemes, is now resolved with clarity and dignity.

In this scheme many threads are drawn together, all of which existed in the work of Mackintosh's British predecessors and contemporaries, but which had never before been combined with such expertise. The plan arrangements and their conformity 58 with structural logic are worthy of Philip Webb;

79

57 *Haus eines Kunstfreundes*. Elevations

OST : WEST

they are as accomplished as the work of Norman Shaw, without his dependence on structural gymnastics for their realisation. The elevations are as studied, in their relation of solid and void, of rhythm and accent, as those of Shaw, and yet the features of which they are composed serve the related internal spaces precisely and accurately. The simplicity and elimination of extraneous detail are derived from Voysey, and yet there is neither Voysey's blandness nor his prettiness. There is as much interest in complex internal space as in Baillie Scott – who was, incidentally, the chief exponent of the 'open plan' – without losing for a moment the control of formal relationships. And finally, the whole composition, inside and out, is firmly bonded and stamped with Mackintosh's fully developed personal graphic vocabulary. It is architectural art of a very high order indeed, and in its urbane elegance and inventiveness is readily comparable with the innovations of that other, earlier Scot, Robert Adam.

But it remained to be proved whether the marvellous virtuosity of the *Haus eines Kunstfreundes* could be produced in a real building, on a real site, and, most inhibiting of all, for a real client.

In 1902 W. W. Blackie, a publisher, was put in touch with Mackintosh by Talwin Morris, a close friend of the architect's who had been associated with him in his graphic enterprises and was now art manager for Blackie's firm. Blackie, having seen Windyhill, offered Mackintosh the commission for a new house, to be built in the town of Helensburgh. Mackintosh naturally accepted, with the unusual but significant insistence that he must spend some time with the family before actually beginning to design on their behalf.

The site is again on a south-sloping hillside overlooking the town and with a splendid view of the Firth of Clyde. It is a much gentler slope than that at Kilmacolm, and the approach road lies to the west, rather than to the north. The general disposition of the plan is much the same as that of Windyhill, although this house, Hill House, as it was named, is noticeably larger, and, in deference to the approach, the main entrance is situated on the end of the building rather than on one of its major faces. The family likeness with Kilmacolm is, moreover, not confined to its plan dispositions. The external materials are also much the same – although the

58 *Haus eines Kunstfreundes.* Plans

59 *Haus eines Kunstfreundes.*
Project for the dining-room.

Opposite
III Hill House, Helensburgh, 1902,
from the south-east.
IV The drawing-room at Hill House.

walling material is a local sandstone rather than whin, in accordance with estate requirements – and their detailing and disposition are in the same vein. The stairwell, standing at right-angles to the main axis of the building in the manner of the *Haus eines Kunstfreundes*, is treated in the same way as both its predecessors. The windows, dormers, chimneys, and gables all betray their provenance.

But there are significant external differences from both earlier houses. While clearly the externals are disposed according to internal demands, there is much more assured control, particularly on the principal faces, than in the Windyhill scheme. Even in the north courtyard, where the complex massing and variegated planning create external demands difficult of resolution, there is more conscious order than on its simpler predecessor at Windyhill. And on the other faces, the distribution of elements is as careful, in its own way, as the *Haus eines Kunstfreundes*. But it is different from the competition scheme as well. It is less urbane, and more overtly Scottish. There is no doubt that in both respects this was intended.

Mackintosh's use of 'history', if his casual references in this building and Windyhill to the Scottish Baronial idiom can so be called, are almost classic examples of their time. The great fondness he expressed in his 1891 paper for his native tradition was characteristic of a similar interest generally among architects who specifically wished to produce

60

something 'modern' for their own time. And it is notable that the historical periods on which all these British architects focused their interest and affection were what might be called 'transitional' periods when flux and change were evident, when the collar of style was worn loosely over the demands of changing function and building methods. Thus the vogue for 'Queen Anne', 'modern Gothic' – very late and very flat, 'Jacobean' and 'Elizabethan', and of course 'Scottish Baronial'. The architects used these styles in a way that might show sympathy without subservience, courtesy without constraint. Thus could the architect, it was hoped, find the sense of direction he so desperately needed, and establish a continuity between the past and the existing environment, without in any sense being bound by it.

Mackintosh's commitment to this principle is clear, both from his writing and from the buildings themselves. Hill House and Windyhill are unmistakably heirs of the Scottish Baronial idiom, without possessing any single feature that has a direct precedent. The elements that are most clearly derivative are such things as the small corner stair tower in the re-entrant angle of the two main wings, yet this is a gesture in kind, not in imitation.

The interior of Hill House is further evidence of progression. Based on Windyhill, it is larger and more complex. The plan is also, at first glance, less clear. In fact it is set out with consummate skill, and the apparent lack of clarity is due to the development that has taken place in Mackintosh's treatment of the individual rooms. In this respect the two most notable rooms are the drawing-room and the main bedroom. Looking at them first in plan, one is struck by the irregularity of outline which may suggest irresolution. In fact the opposite is true. The drawing-room contains two large recesses. One of these is a bay projecting out of the south face of the building, rather like the Windyhill prototype,

V A cabinet for Mrs Rowat.
University of Glasgow. Mackintosh
Collection.
VI White painted chair
and table *c*. 1900.

63 *Opposite*. Hill House. The
entrance gates.

64 Hill House. Window alcove in the drawing-room.

but larger and more sharply delineated. It contains a built-in seat and two doors leading to the garden. The concentration of light from the expanse of glass is in notable contrast to the fireplace end, the 'winter' end of the room, which is served by a single, smaller window. The other major recess was designed to receive a studio piano or to serve as an informal stage for the small theatrical performances in which the younger members of the family like to engage. There is a nominal cornice or picture rail running around the room, familiar from Mackintosh's earlier interiors, from which the main ceiling rises some three feet. The underside of this rail establishes the ceiling levels in the alcoves and determines the height of doors. The higher central 'drum' thus defined, was painted in a very dark sombre colour. The final effect of this treatment is that the main proportion of the room is clearly established, and the resultant panels of doors, walls, and alcoves are allowed an easy fluidity.

The main bedroom, again, derives its apparently irregular shape from its pattern of use. The bed is placed in a large alcove off the main rectangle of the room, on the same pattern as, but on a less lavish scale than, the bedroom in the *Haus eines Kunstfreundes*. Here too, the same ceiling device is used for defining and linking the spaces, although between the high ceiling level and the lower line of the door, wardrobe, and window heads an intermediate element is introduced. The bed alcove has a barrel-vaulted ceiling which springs from the lower level and just touches the higher. This definition of the precise functional allocations within rooms, both in plan and section, followed by the design of fixed and free furniture, gives an extraordinary sensation of organic wholeness; but because of the real grasp and control of the actual functioning of the rooms, they do not have the oppressive immobility often associated with this degree of architectural autonomy. People, curiously enough, are not out of place

within them, although it must be acknowledged that certain kinds of furniture would be.

Over the sequence of house designs considered here, a progression, an increasing refinement of intent can be seen. It is possible, however, to feel that the step from the *Haus eines Kunstfreundes* to Hill House was slightly retrogressive. The latter is more overtly historical in that it is notably more tied to tradition and less completely pictorially resolved in its exterior treatment. But apart from the fact that it is always easier to resolve such a scheme pictorially when there is no building budget and no demanding dialogue with a real client, there is every evidence that Mackintosh welcomed the actual exigencies of the real situation as the generators of 'real' architecture, as mentioned in relation to the Art School scheme. The idea, emanating from the Ruskin and Morris ideologies, of the production of a building as a social process and not a single creative act was with him a firm principle. It was a particularly 'social' process in the case of Hill House, for the Blackie family had an unexpected addition to their family during the course of construction; Mackintosh responded with rare sympathy by creating a nursery at the polar extreme from the master's study.

During the three years (1900–02) in which this series of domestic designs emerged, other events were occurring. The first of these, an event which had the air of the inevitable about it, was his marriage on August 22nd, 1900 to Margaret Macdonald. There has been, inevitably, a good deal of idle speculation about the marriage and its effect on the architect's development, and there can be no doubt that Margaret, posthumously, fell prey to the ironies of history. Those critics, starting with P. Morton Shand in his *Architectural Review* articles in 1935, who saw Mackintosh solely as an antecedent of the International Style, and for whom the sole criteria of merit were rectangularity and the absence

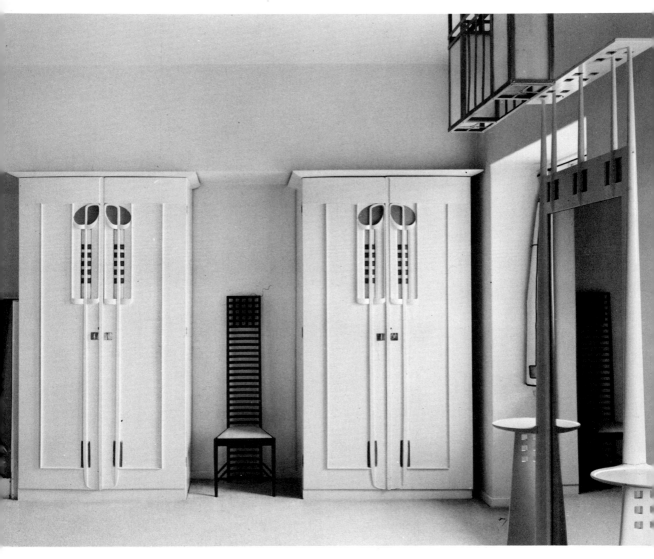

of ornament, found in Margaret the scapegoat for the decorative predilections in Mackintosh's work which they could neither comprehend nor accept. And so, it has been suggested, she impeded him in his unconscious progress towards a 20th-century ideal.

There is, emphatically, no evidence whatever to support this idea. There is every evidence that he appreciated and encouraged her decorative activities, and that she, in her turn, acknowledged and encouraged his vastly greater gifts. Further, she provided him in a life which became increasingly demanding with much needed support. His personality from the beginning was not marked by stability, and the high bounding enthusiasm and garrulous discussion had their opposites in intense depression and brooding silence. Her constancy and support were unflagging, and their devotion was mutual.

In these early years there was little need of encouragement, with plenty of work at home, and a growing following abroad. The *Dekorative Kunst* article of 1898 had been Mackintosh's introduction to the Continent, and this was followed in the year of his marriage by an invitation to furnish and decorate a room, together with the MacNairs, in the 8th Secessionist Exhibition in Vienna. The bulk of the exhibits were borrowed from work already executed for Glasgow clients. Charles and Margaret went to Vienna, and both they and their work were enthusiastically acclaimed, apparently by critics and public alike, and the triumph was followed by contributions to exhibitions in a number of European centres over the following years. These exhibitions in themselves are not central to the study of Mackintosh's development; they demonstrate Mackintosh's facility in adapting essentially unsuitable space to his own visual requirements, but their constituents were either taken from, or virtually identical to, those he was producing for his clients at home. They brought him into contact with the leaders of change abroad,

69, 70 Hill House. Designs for the principal
bedroom, west and south walls. University of
Glasgow. Mackintosh Collection.
71 *Opposite.* The staircase at Hill House.

72 Design for a cabinet for Mrs Rowat. University of Glasgow. Mackintosh Collection.

72 Design for a cabinet for Mrs Rowat. University of Glasgow. Mackintosh Collection.

although, with only one exception, this contact was regrettably on the basis of interior decoration, and not architecture.

That one exception was the *Haus eines Kunstfreundes*, which was published by Koch. This was sufficient to isolate Mackintosh from the other Scottish designers as not only an inventive decorator, but an architect of originality and power. In spite of the masterly quality of the *Haus eines Kunstfreundes* scheme, it is unfortunate that this, rather than his realised buildings, should have been his architectural introduction to Europe. For without an understanding of the designer's background and evolution to this point, it was bound to give a misleading impression. Even Muthesius, who of all Europeans should have understood something of its antecedents, said of the scheme: 'The exterior architecture of the building . . . exhibits an absolutely original character, unlike anything else known. In it we shall not find a trace of the conventional forms of architecture, to

which the artist, so far as his present intentions were concerned, was quite indifferent.' This was simply not true, although it is easy to see how the design, taken in isolation, could give something of that impression.

Of the various interior design and furnishing commissions executed during these years, it must be noted that all suffered from the initial disadvantage of the exhibition work; that of having to adapt to the strictures of existing buildings. Much could be done, and much was ingeniously done, to alter the visual scale of unsuitable ceiling heights and to mask or alter unsuitable features, but ultimately none of them could have expressed so fully either the architect's intentions or his powers as the interiors of Hill House. It was here, in a building whose every detail was under his direct charge, whose client had real needs and yet every sympathy, that the synthesis of Mackintosh's skills and intentions can first be really felt, and the measure of his genius first appreciated.

CHAPTER SIX 1901-1904

'(The artist) must possess technical invention in order to create for himself suitable processes of expression – and above all he requires the aid of invention in order to transform the elements with which nature supplies him – and compose new images from them.'

Writing on the subject of 'Seemliness', Mackintosh tried to sum up his own artistic motivations during these early years of his maturity. And it is this idea of transformation that enabled him to reconcile his acknowledged subservience to Nature with the increasingly abstracted and inventive forms which characterised his work. It was noted that on one occasion he had used the dissected eye of a fish as the theme for decorative exercise, but the principle he was trying to establish here went rather further than the imitation of obscure natural forms. 'The artist may have a very rich psychic organisation – an easy grasp and a clear eye for essentials – a great variety of aptitudes – but that which characterises him above all else – and determines his vocation – is the exceptional development of the imaginative faculties – especially the imagination that creates – not only the imagination that represents. The power which the artist possesses of representing objects to himself explains the hallucinating character of his work – the poetry which pervades them – and their tendency towards symbolism – but the creative imagination is far more important. The artist cannot attain to mastery in his art unless he is endowed in the highest degree with the faculty of invention.'

He had, of course, established already the principle that this creative effort must not only be stimulated by nature, but must grow out of function: 'The only true modern individual art in proportion in form and in colour, is produced by an emotion, produced by a frank and intelligent understanding of the absolute and true requirements of a building or object – a scientific knowledge of the possibilities and beauties of material, a fearless application of emotion and knowledge, a cultured intelligence, and a mind artistic yet not too indolent to attempt the task of clothing in grace and beauty the new forms and conditions that modern development of life – social, commercial, and religious, insist upon.'

It is this curious interlocking of intellect and emotion, of function and fantasy, that gives to all his works, but particularly to his interior designs, their fascinating flavour. This is particularly true of the tea-room projects for Miss Cranston, over which, after 1901, he had sole professional control. In 1901 he began work on Miss Cranston's premises in Ingram Street, Glasgow. These comprised an extensive collection of rooms, to which she added by acquiring leases of adjoining properties. Mackintosh was commissioned to design the interior for the latest of these acquisitions, followed after a lapse of several years by the redesigning of the earlier rooms.

The first of these rooms, the white dining-room, is in spirit and detail much like his domestic interiors. But the detail is simpler and more robust, although there is the same attenuated verticality, and the use of thin, flat horizontals as a counter-measure. In terms of 'creative imagination' – as Mackintosh used the words – it is subtly, but not signally different from the domestic interiors of this period.

To see the changes which he could ring with this application of imagination, it is necessary to compare this interior with those for Miss Cranston that followed, in 1902–4 at the Willow Tea-Rooms in Sauchiehall Street. But it is important to preface this comparison with the fact that these later rooms cannot be taken to represent a stylistic 'advance'; they were merely imaginatively 'different', for a different set of commercial circumstances. The Willow Tea-Rooms were contained in an entirely new building designed by Mackintosh; there were five separate dining or tea-rooms, a dining gallery, and a billiards room. The three major dining-rooms, or spaces, were open to one another and in all the

73 The Willow Tea-rooms, Sauchiehall Street, Glasgow. 1902–4. The façade.

furnishings were the same. But by his use of the space, the lighting, and the decorative fittings the difference in quality between rooms can be deduced even from pictures. And their collective contrast with the fourth room, the Room de Luxe, is even more marked. It can, of course, be argued that these theatricalities were a trivial side issue for a serious architect to undertake, but it cannot be argued so from Mackintosh's own testimony. For these rooms, collectively, demonstrate quite clearly the principles – if so they can be called – that he was attempting to lay down in his lecture. They also demonstrate some other points from that lecture. He referred to the use of 'symbolism' in the arts. The whole of the Willow Tea-Rooms were detailed around an elaborate play on the willow-tree form, from which the street name, Sauchiehall, had been derived. Not only was the willow-leaf used as a motif throughout the decoration, but clearly the abstracted forms of the decorative ironwork, the plaster friezes, and the various fittings were given an imagery relating, however distantly, to tree shapes. The culmination of this 'symbolism' was the gesso panel by Margaret Mackintosh inspired by Rossetti's sonnet 'O ye, all ye that walk in willow wood', mounted in the Room de Luxe.

Providing the context for this decorative virtuosity was the spatial enclosure of the building itself. Here, for the only time, was Mackintosh able to provide the actual enclosure, and the way in which he shaped and related the spaces is of considerable interest. It was a typical commercial site, facing north on to one of the city's major shopping centres, narrow, deep, and bounded on either side by large, typical buildings.

The building was four storeys high, for half the depth from the main street, and storey-and-a-half, or single storey with gallery, in the rear. This gallery extended from the first landing, about two-thirds of the vertical distance between ground and

74 Tall chairs of stained wood, with drop-in seats and pierced oval backrail, as exhibited by Mackintosh at the Secessionist Exhibition in Vienna of 1900.

first floors, and extended around the perimeter of
the rear part of the building. A large sky-light in
the roof of this portion illuminated both the gallery,
75 and through the well, the dining-room below. The
main stair connecting these spaces was not enclosed,
nor was the front edge of the gallery below the
ground-floor ceiling. These three major spaces and
the stair were thus entirely open to one another and the
articulation between them achieved by the disposition
of floors and ceilings rather than by walls.

Much has been made of Mackintosh's play with
space as a positive architectural element, and in this
building as much as in any of his work, it is easy to
see what is meant. But although his manipulation
and control were masterly, it would be incautious to
use this as a characteristic which set him aside from
his contemporaries. It was, after all, a characteristic
of both Gothic and Baroque architecture, of Piranesi's
prison engravings, of the Crystal Palace, and of any
number of Victorian industrial or commercial
structures where space was divided for separate,
though still public, functions. It was, too, a prime
characteristic, and a conscious one, of the all-popular
Baillie Scott domestic interiors, and it may fairly
be said that Scott displayed far more conscious
interest in 'open planning' than Mackintosh ever did.

Nonetheless, Mackintosh did exploit its possibilities brilliantly. One of the contributory factors to
the visual interest was his treatment of detail. For
his predilection for line and linear ornament tended
to give an impression of direction and of surface,
but not of mass. Take, for example, his repeated
use of simple board-and-batten panelling on walls
as in the white dining-room at Ingram Street or the
sub-gallery dining-room at Sauchiehall Street.
Whereas conventional panelling contains horizontal
members with the verticals, thus framing each panel,
and the panels themselves are bevelled into the frame,
accentuating their proportion and dimension, these
are simply linear repeats, slashed by horizontals

76 The Willow Tea-rooms.
Wrought iron balustrade.

Opposite
VII Willow Tea-rooms. The door of
the Room de Luxe. 1902–4.

which are detailed in such a way as to delimit the vertical lines without in any way creating closed forms. This avoidance of closed forms, of static proportions, can be seen too in the vertical stair rods replacing the conventional handrail and balustrading, by the exposed beam-and-joint system in the ground-floor ceiling even to the extent of bringing the joist ends out into the perimeter of the open well, and the beams right through it as though that well were not a fixed and immutable entity but merely an arbitrary interruption of a linear system.

It is by this treatment, now so familiar in architecture, that the great dynamic illusion of spatial 'interpenetration' is achieved. But it must be noted that the same characteristic applies where there is no intimation of space whatever. For instance, the exteriors of his houses, which are essentially flat surfaces, are given the same kind of flat linear scoring. Here, there is no illusion of 'interpenetration' for there is no attempt to create an ambiguity

77 Three characteristic Mackintosh chairs, with markedly disproportionate heights of back. The tall chair with pierced splats was used in the Ingram Street tea-rooms of 1901.

78 A pair of sturdy, low barrel-shaped chairs with tiered table as used in the games-rooms of the Cranston tea-rooms.

between solid and void as, for instance, was beginning to appear in Frank Lloyd Wright's houses of the same period. In Mackintosh's houses the voids are unambiguously, albeit erratically, disposed; the solid masses, however, are bent and broken in such a way as to deny any identifiable closed geometry. To use an analogy with which he would have been sympathetic, it is an organic rather than a crystalline geometry, the indeterminacy of growing things.

The organic analogy is, of course, one that Mackintosh used himself, and it is easy enough to see how both the approach and the technique were related to his developed graphic techniques and to his neo-Gothic preferences. But there was another underlying reason, one that he hinted at in his lecture on 'Seemliness': '. . . you will never learn to walk so long as there are props. The props of art are – on the one hand – the slavish imitation of old work – no matter what date or from what country – and on the other hand the absurd and false idea – that there can be any living emotion expressed in work scientifically proportioned according to ancient principles – but clothed in the thin fantasy of the author's own fancy.'

D

Opposite
VIII Glasgow School of Art.
The west façade, 1907–9.

This prop of ancient proportional principles was becoming at this time a lively issue, and was one of the signs of the growing affection for a disciplined and codified architectural framework for design. It was the general and inevitable reaction of order against chaos, but it was one that Mackintosh, in the certainty and mastery of his own freedom, bitterly opposed. This opposition was even apparent in an area of design where it would appear to be impossible – in the design of furniture.

Of the two basic types of chair seen in the tea-rooms – and throughout his work – one was low and more or less cubical, and the other was extremely tall. Many of his chairs of the first type were, in fact based on the cube, that simplest and most static of proportional forms, but the constituent parts were assembled as lapping planes, maintaining their separate identity. The very tall chairs, which tended to be more conventional in their assembly, were nonetheless so attenuated as to make them entirely linear objects, and to deny any determinate relationship between, say, seat and back. This is easily established by comparing two similar chairs in which the height of the backs differs by several inches; a variation which in conventional chairs would have a critical visual effect becomes quite irrelevant. Similarly in his fondness for thin, overlapping planes as tops for tables, chests of drawers, and indeed buildings, the emphasis is entirely on surface and plane rather than on any precise proportional relationship with the other parts of the assembly.

But Mackintosh's interest in line and surface must not be confused with the latter-day preoccupation with extreme lightness and structural virtuosity. In a paper addressed to a literary society, undated, but probably from four to five years after the turn of the century, he discussed architecture under the three traditional heads of strength, usefulness, and beauty. In view of the historical position Mackintosh has come to assume, it is worth quoting at length

his views on 'strength or stability'. 'This quality or condition refers to good sound practical workmanship in all the materials, which materials must vary with the locality. Strength itself will be a criterion of the excellency of the architecture, everything approaching the gimcrack or flimsy will condemn the building be it ever so lovely. Of course this does not mean that a summer-house or conservatory be built like a fortress, but it demands that all noble ornament should be of the most enduring material, and placed in the most secure positions. So much in architecture (is) dependent on the quality that it requires not only the real fact but the appearance and will prefer of two equally substantial materials the one which has the most bulk. I think that you will admit that it is the want of bulk which is the chief blemish of modern street architecture. Iron is much stronger than stone and so a thin clothes pole of metal is as strong as a much bulkier piece of stone or brick but the eye is distressed at huge lofty tenements resting to all appearance on nothing more stable than plate-glass for the real actual supports are easily overlooked.

'These two comparatively modern materials, iron and glass, though eminently suitable for many purposes will never worthily take the place of stone because of this defect – the want of mass. With the advent of the Crystal Palace and the many rose-tinted hallucinations of that period arose the belief in the invention of a new style. At last common-sense, it was shouted, prevails – no more connections with the works of the past – no more deference to the ideas of artists, poets, or even the principles of beauty in nature; for now we can pile up the hugest buildings with the least possible means of support, and that on most economical principles as design can be turned out of the foundry without limit, to the minimising of intellectual labour and so also to the payment of it. But time has passed, and practical experience has shown that apart altogether

107

79 Slender white painted armchair with linen covered drop-in seat. The back panel is also linen covered and printed with a stencilled flower motif. Chairs of this type were exhibited both at Vienna and Turin in 1902.

from any defect in stability or actual comfort the want of appearance of stability is fatal to the introduction of such a style for either domestic, civil, or ecclesiastical buildings. These demand actual mass even if of a weaker material taking bulk for bulk. The leaning tower of Pisa though abundantly strong as has been proved by centuries, is yet tottering and insecure to all appearance, some say so much as that to sleep under its tottering shadow would be almost impossible. Thus in this quality of architecture mind and body must be considered. Egyptian remains will always impress the mind in a way Chinese flippery never will. The Alhambra, gorgeous and refined in its ornament though it was, more beautiful than perhaps any other building, yet because its materials are but plaster, wood, porcelain and tile work, is yet of a lower type of architecture than the far plainer but more enduring country churches of England or Normandy.'

It would be well, then, to pass on that note from the Willow Tea-Rooms – Mackintosh's 'Alhambra' – to his 1903 submission for the Liverpool Cathedral competition. It is, whatever else, massive. It is also in its plan, disposition, structure, and materials, entirely traditional. Within this traditional framework, the forms and details are firmly within, and directly derived from, the 'modern Gothic' idiom, although in their outworking they would doubtless be stamped with the characteristic Mackintosh flavour. There is no evidence here – nor is there any in his writing – to suggest any ideological change from the time of the Queen's Cross project, or even, perhaps, the Soane medallion design of the railway terminus, although there is much more competence and a clearer purpose. And, by comparison, the scheme is less adventurous than the submission of Lethaby and E. S. Prior, and even less so than Bentley's Westminster Cathedral in London, then nearing completion.

So the picture of Mackintosh as a conscious pioneer of modernity must be carefully qualified. He was certainly firmly committed to the principle of producing an architecture of his own time; he was quite prepared to break with precedent to serve a new function or explore a new imagery; he was violently opposed to any suggestion of historical mummery. But he was equally committed to preserving a visible and meaningful continuity with the past, to using old materials in the old ways, and to respecting old conventions for old functions.

Mackintosh discussed, in the foregoing paper, at some length the problem of beauty in architecture, and it reveals a good deal about not only his attitudes but the buildings themselves. He began by foundering nobly on the rock of 'taste'. This effort though admittedly unsuccessful was not without significance, for there were two contemporary ways of dealing with the problem, either one of which would have navigated him past it. One was the attitude of the Lethaby group, from William Morris, which saw in the very concept of 'taste' the distillation of all that was wrong with contemporary attitudes towards culture. They maintained simply that it did not or should not exist beyond entirely rational appropriateness; that any idea of a special 'gift' or cultivated sensibility beyond the thorough and workmanlike exploration of defined problems was a snare and a snobbish delusion. The other school seemed in many respects virtually to confirm the objections of the first. For they, admitting with Ruskin this special sensibility, and yet despairing of its definition, fell back on history. They saw in, or read into the past, and most readily the past of the Renaissance, convenient canons which could be learned, taught, and which could provide cultural anchors in the world of volcanic change which surrounded them.

Mackintosh rejected both. And it was this rejection which, as much as any other factor, isolated him from the support and approbation of his British contemporaries. He deplored the reversion to outmoded rules, yet he would allow of neither anarchy in matters of taste, nor of its unconscious assimilation: 'The faculty of distinguishing good from bad in design is a faculty which most educated people – and especially ladies – conceive they possess. How it has been acquired few would be able to explain. The general impression seems to be that it is the peculiar inheritance of gentle blood, and independent of all training that while a young lady is devoting at school, or under a governess, so many hours a day to music, so many to languages, and so many to general science, she is all the time unconsciously forming that sense of the beautiful which we call taste, that the sense once developed will enable her unassisted by any special study or experience not only to appreciate the charms of nature in every aspect, but to form a correct estimate of the merits of works in architecture, painting, sculpture, etc. That this impression had gained ground may be inferred from the fact that there is no single point on which well-educated women are more jealous of disparagement than in this. We may condemn a lady's opinion in politics – criticise her handwriting – correct her pronunciation of Latin and disparage her favourite authors with a chance of escaping displeasure, but if we venture to question her taste in the most trivial matter we are sure to offend.'

The argument is good, although the statement was not original. He was quoting C. L. Eastlake. Yet he was insistent that this 'sense of the beautiful' had a real and objective existence. This reality was to be discovered through certain 'principles of beauty which are common to . . . all true beauty'.

The first of these was 'truth'. And truth in architecture 'is only present when every material is shown on its own merits and mimics not the resem-blance of any others. Thus it may be necessary in a brick wall to weather-proof it – internally or exter-nally it does not matter – with plaster or cement which may be done and no deceit shown but the practice is detestable where it is scored over to delude into the belief that stone is used.' He then went on to discuss the use of other veneering and finishing materials – gilding and marble veneering were acceptable because of the well-understood costliness of the materials, and thus no sham was implicit, paint was to be used on woodwork in preference to graining, and an even better solution was the use of coloured stains revealing the actual grain of the material. Cast-iron 'can be a useful and at the same time beautiful object, but it is not improved when with imitation rivet heads it tries to pass for hand-wrought metal work or by paint for bronze'.

But matters such as these were 'but the auxiliaries of architecture'. The same principle when applied to the fundamentals of architectural design forbade such frauds as he had deplored on his youthful visit to Siena, and such devices as the erection of tall gables before low-pitched roofs, 'gables that are simply masks, not the decoration and expressions of the necessities of the buildings, but to meet the supposed requirements of the Gothic style they are lofty and steeply pitched, so that only a view from another point of view than that intended by the architect discloses the sham'. Wren's St Paul's duly received its traditional moral censure for its 'false' upper storey, and he then went on to define another principle of 'beauty'.

'. . . that construction should be decorated, and not decoration constructed. . . . Thus the salient and most requisite features should be selected for orna-mentation, so from this it must appear that, windows and doors being about the most important of modern requirements, round these should any ornament be sought. Yet note how this is forgotten in a type of building you are all acquainted with – the classic churches in vogue 20 years ago . . . which you will note depend for architectural effect on the application of flat columns attached to the walls in imitation of the temple style, while the windows and doors are simply holes in the walls – observe I am not com-plaining of plainness when little money can be got but of misapplication of money when obtained.' And so he went on with the kind of Puginesque argument that had been familiar for half a century or more.

His next principle was one which, in view of his work, may be somewhat surprising: 'Yet one other powerful element in Beauty is association or tradition, which will modify the force of laws which in the abstract are admitted to be correct and true and grant a certain . . . to local or national customs or to practices sanctioned of high authority. When Burns in his *Cotter's Saturday Night* after enumerating some of our favourite psalm tunes burst out 'com-pared wae they Italian trills are tame', as a piece of musical criticism it may not hold true world-wide yet it is a very sufficient reason and obvious truth to Scotsmen, so in the same manner there are many decorative features in Scotch architecture, which might well be replaced by others of antiquity yet just because we are Scotch and not Greek or Roman we reject. For example there is the quaint old Scotch gate pillars with the spire resting on 3 or 4 stone bullets – the curious balls often seen at stairs . . . and very many other features which give a historical character to the buildings they adorn. . . . In fact I think we should be a little less cosmopolitan and rather more national in our architecture, as we are with language, new words and phrases will be incorporated gradually, but the wholesale intro-duction of Japanese sentiment for example would be denounced and rightly by the purist.'

But then, having admitted the role of the tradi-tional, he had to give an immediate corrective: 'Still of course this conservatism is often made a cloak for and excuse for mediocrity in design and the causeless and unceasing repetition of features which have only their age to recommend them; and so Variety and Novelty if not carried too far, are qualities both allowable and desirable, but by ignorance often clamoured for most unreasonably.'

The inadequacy of his argument is a fair reflection of the quandary of the times. But the very points he raised as principles of beauty were those that had motivated the whole post-Pugin phase of the Gothic Revival, and through the whole of this argument, as through all of his writing, his affection for the Gothic is clear. At one point in his lecture he

82 Liverpool Cathedral. South elevation

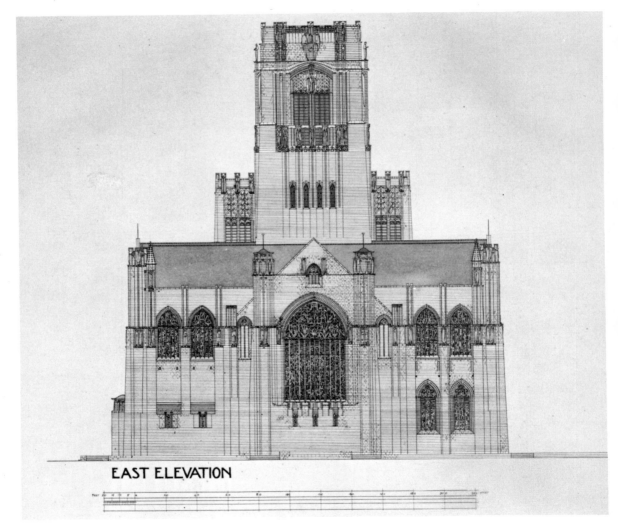

83 Liverpool Cathedral. East elevation

EAST ELEVATION

even mentioned with favour Sir Gilbert Scott's treatment of St Mary's Cathedral in Edinburgh. This, of course, did not make him a Gothic Revivalist; but the firm allegiance to these principles, the self-evident way in which they influenced his work, and his confessed admiration for the leading figures in that succession, place him clearly and precisely in the British picture. Why then was he not recognised and acclaimed within it? There are a number of contributory answers, but their force was not to be appreciated until after 1910 when his full development was realised in the completion of the Art School, and when, tragically, his effective architectural output was finished.

114

CHAPTER SEVEN 1904-1909

In 1904 John Honeyman retired and Mackintosh became an official partner in the firm, thenceforth known as Honeyman, Keppie and Mackintosh. It seems clear that relations within the firm were amicable enough, although there is no evidence to suggest any degree of intimacy between Mackintosh and either of his senior partners, in spite of the fact that Keppie was only six years older. Nor is there any evidence in the work of the firm that Mackintosh's personal style had any marked effect on other projects. Since the time of the competition for the Art School, however, it is clear that he had considerable or complete autonomy in the projects assigned to him. Indeed, in view of his considerable independent success, it is, unthinkable that he would have remained in the firm had this not been the case.

After the Liverpool Cathedral competition scheme, Mackintosh began work on a new Glasgow school. Scottish primary and secondary education was generally acknowledged, with that of Germany, to have the most advanced national level in Europe, and a fundamental policy of Scottish education, unlike that of England, was that it should be co-educational. The school that Mackintosh designed represented the usual Scottish pattern, comprising a collection of class-rooms, a large assembly and drill hall, a cookery class-room, and lavatory and cloak-room facilities ranked beside the separate stair towers for each sex. The simple, direct bifurcation of the plan is the direct acknowledgement of this most symmetrical of programmes.

The stringent cost controls exercised then, as now, on school building are reflected not only by the economy of the plan but in the elimination of extraneous detail inside and outside the finished building. Such decorative detail as there is has been concentrated, in accordance with his expressed theory, around doors and windows. And while the forms, by hindsight can be taken, and have been taken, as extremely prophetic of the new architecture, they belong, in their essence, equally with the building forms of their own time. Perhaps not surprisingly, in trying to exploit what Mackintosh called 'the spirit of the old' without slavishly emulating its details, he produced a building with the 'spirit of the new'. Indeed, it could fairly be said that the construction of the walls, the framing around window openings, the forms of the roofs and the building materials are all in accord with those of the tenement buildings 84 which had become, notoriously, the main building fabric of the city during the 19th century. What transform their use in this instance are, the clear and orderly disposition of the plan elements expressed in 85 the building form, the size and proportions of the windows in response to the functional needs, and the precise visual relationships established by this master graphic artist.

It is worth speculating on the different image Mackintosh might have presented to the world had his two major monuments, aside from domestic building, not been educational establishments severely strictured by cost. It is certain that his reputation would not have been less, and probably would have been in his own time considerably greater, but it would also have been somewhat different. For the decorative restraint that characterises these buildings, and which made such critics as Gleeson White hail him as a prophet of machine age architecture, was to Mackintosh a question of what Pugin called 'propriety'. Scotland Street School represented one end of a social hierarchy whose other end, and whose pinnacle, was represented by Liverpool Cathedral, and the rich iconography and decorative embellishment of the one was as valid a social response as the restraint of the other.

During the period from initial design to the completion of construction of the Scotland Street School, that is from 1903 to 1906, Mackintosh was engaged in the construction of the Willow Tea-Rooms, and in the conversion and interior design

115

84 Scotland Street School.
Exterior. 1903–6.
85 *Opposite*. Scotland Street School.
Interior of entrance bay.

of a large house for Miss Cranston and her husband, Major Cochrane.

In the decorations for this house, there are no appreciable differences in principle from the domestic interiors of the previous years, or from the tea-room designs. The work consisted primarily of refurbishing and refurnishing existing interiors, and while many of the bits he designed had the expected ingenuity and originality, in only one instance was he able to manipulate the interior space itself. This was in the music room, whose one end, as existing, was semi-circular in plan. He exploited this by poising a flat horizontal member – rather like his usual picture rail – in a continuous circle concentric with, and some two feet within, the end wall. This member was supported on the room side by a screen of vertical slats for a segment of its length, and on the curved-wall side by typical built-in fittings, benches and window seats. It is a characteristic instance of his demarcation of functional areas within a single space, and if a little more overt than in the earlier domestic interiors, may well have been due to his experience with larger scaled spatial relationships at the Willow Tea-Rooms.

There exist two brief accounts of meetings with Mackintosh during this period, when he was in his middle thirties, and at the height of his success. The first, by E. B. Kalas, was published in *De la Tamise à la Sprée: L'essor des industries d'art* in 1905. Kalas went, as on a pilgrimage, to meet the Mackin-toshes in their flat in 120 Mains Street, Glasgow. His style is florid, and his tone eulogising, but the description is of interest: 'Meet . . . the occupants of this house of white and violet. A gentleman, thirty-five years old, tall, dressed all in black, with long dark hair parted in the middle; the eyes slumber in their setting of bushy eyebrows but flame up from their gloom in occasional flashes of vari-coloured sparks; the mouth betrays caution, perhaps timidity – probably mockery. The general appearance is of a

clean-shaven American clergyman who is still pulsing with the emotion and travail of his last metaphysical discourse but has succeeded, by powers of restraint, in preserving an impassivity and an unnatural silence – Charles Rennie Mackintosh.' He was probably not far off the mark. The other, by Desmond Chapman-Huston, was written in retrospect from 1949, and marked the first meeting of what was to become a lifelong friendship. The one personal observation that Chapman-Huston made was that he immediately and instinctively felt himself to be in the presence of a great man; whether the impression was the creation of memory cannot be known. But it does seem clear that this strong vein of brooding intensity was even then sufficiently marked to set him apart in the minds of those who met him. Chapman-Huston recalled also a reference by Charles to his wife's work: 'Margaret has genius; I have only talent.' The myopia of love is a common enough phenomenon; nevertheless the sentiment bespeaks more than a reluctant toleration of her decorative enterprises.

In establishing an accurate chronology of design for such an architect as Mackintosh, it is important to realise the sometimes considerable duration of time required for building and the consequent overlap of one scheme with another. This constructional overlap is of some importance, for to a man of his design philosophy, the designing process never stopped until the builder had literally left the premises. Thus, for example, Hill House was not actually completed until the spring of 1904, by which time the Willow tea-rooms were under way, the Liverpool Cathedral scheme was over a year behind, and the Scotland Street School design work had begun. Concurrently, a number of decorative commissions had been and were being carried out. It was a period of intense – in view of the attention he lavished on his work, phenomenally intense – production, and the climax by which history knows him began in the following year, 1905, with the design revisions for the completion of the Art School.

The startling changes that emerged in the completion of this building in 1909 reveal both the changes that had taken place in Mackintosh's personal manner over the decade since the first design, and those principles which were the underlying, and unchanging, constants in his work.

The only parts of this west wing which remained substantially unchanged from the initial scheme were the major north-facing studios and their elevation to the street. For the rest, some changes were the result of functional requirements, and some merely the detailed outworking of his mature style and his accumulated experience.

One of the weaknesses in the original scheme which, at this stage, had to be corrected, was the inadequacy of escape stairs in case of fire. He accordingly introduced two new stairs in the re-entrant angles at each end of the south face, one of which had of course to be connected to the existing structure. This easternmost stair passed by and obstructed two of the existing windows to the original Board Room on the first floor. In his quixotic treatment

of this problem can be seen his attachment to the Arts and Crafts principle of building design as a social document – that it should tell in its fabric not only of the needs that brought it into being, but of the changing circumstances of its history and adaptation. Rather than remove the windows, which could no longer serve the room with light, and which in any event were shallow protruding bays which obstructed the clear run of the stair, he carefully left them in place, with obscured glass, and tortuously formed the run of treads around them.

The south elevation, abutting and overhanging a miscellaneous collection of buildings – then and now – is an agglomeration of such responses to the calls of 'nature'; there are minor elements which preserve a tenuous, though half-hearted acknowledgment of symmetry, but they are overwhelmed by the enthusiastic accretions called into being by change. An extra storey was incorporated in this second stage, providing masters' studios; it created a problem of access to alternate staircases, since the existing Director's studio effectively barred passage from one end to the other. Mackintosh solved the problem by building the upper two storeys of the new wing to the full depth of the floors below, and then

91
92

120

90 Hous'hill. Design for a bedroom. 1903–6

Opposite
IX Glasgow School of Art. The Library

spanning the gap behind the Director's studio with a
93 cantilevered gallery, known as the 'hen-run' and
94 looking for all the world like a segment of a tram-car
tacked on to the face of the building. So it went,
inventing, adapting, creating, with a compulsive
restlessness that makes the whole assembly a warren
of discovery.

What this process cost the clients in patience and
money can only be guessed at, but it was probably
only the support of Newbery that made the adven-
ture possible. What it cost the builders in exaspera-
tion and ingenuity will never be known either, but
there are two occasions when tradesmen downed
tools at the demands the architect was making of
them. One of these was in connection with the
plastering of ogival-shaped corridor-ceiling light
wells, and the other, the execution of complex linear
knots in the ends of wrought iron tee-beams which
protruded into one of the minor studios. Since each
of these knots was different, and they occurred
roughly every six feet for the length of the studio,
the objections can be understood, and it is a tribute
of a sort that the architect not only succeeded in
persuading the workmen to return in both cases, but
to carry out the details as intended.

In connection with this unremitting inventiveness,
however, there are two characteristics that stand out
unusually forcibly. First, no matter how outrageous
the distortion, the decorative details always spring
from some functional or constructional demand –

they are 'decorated construction'. Second, for all the
spaces in the building which are not set aside for
prestige reasons – such as the Board Room – the
materials he exposed and played with are almost
perversely crude. He used rough sawn timber,
exposed, plated and rivetted steel and iron structural
members, rough brickwork, and trowelled but
unfinished cement rendering. The fact that the elimination of some of the wilder details might well have
paid for more ordinary and perhaps pretentious
finishes is irrelevant. He was dramatically exploiting
a state of ruthless economy, even if in a somewhat
uneconomical manner, and the resulting interiors
have a rugged workmanlike quality entirely in keep-
ing with their function fifty years since.

But one of the interior spaces where wet canvases
and plaster droppings would not intrude was the
library, and it is here that the case for Mackintosh
the pioneer of modernism finally focuses. The room
is basically as indicated on the 1896 drawings, a
thirty-five foot square some seventeen feet high, or
two-thirds of the height of the studios. An open
gallery encircles the upper part of the room, creating
within the square of the room a slightly oblong open
well. But whereas the gallery on the original drawings was conventionally supported from below, the
supporting structure and all the detailed handling
that springs from it are, in the finished product,
entirely different.

The finished gallery is supported by two rows of

91, 92 Glasgow School of Art. The east staircase, passing the window of the original Board Room, and below, the east staircase at first floor level.
93 *Opposite*. Glasgow School of Art. The 'loggia' and 'hen-run'.

columns running east and west, and extending upwards to provide support for the ceiling above. The rows of columns are equally spaced across the room, that is between eleven and twelve feet apart, but the galleries are only some eight feet deep – the space required for their function. As a result, the gallery beams are extended outward in pairs to grip the columns, as it were, in space. It is a structural play that has raised inevitable, and often excited, comment. But, not immediately obvious, there is a sound structural reason for the arrangement, and it springs from the fact that the library is but one apartment in a structure of several storeys.

In the cross-section through the library wing the construction of the two floors immediately below the library can be seen as consisting of pairs of steel beams spanning east to west, creating three equal spans for the wood joist floors. The lines of these beams were, in fact, the only reasonable points from which the library gallery could be supported, and the positions from which structural continuity could be established with the floors above. This simple reason for the basic structural system detracts in no

X, XI *Willow Herb,* Buxted, 1919 and below, *Larkspur,* Walberswick, August 1914. Watercolours in the University of Glasgow. Mackintosh Collection.

94 *Opposite.* Exterior view of 'hen-run'.

WILLOW
HERB
BUXSTEAD
1 9 1 9
C R M M M M

LARKSPUR
WALBERSWICK
AUGUST 1914
C.R.M.M.M.M.

way from the visual drama which Mackintosh has then built around his solution, but it does justify according to his own principles a detail which might otherwise be seen as a purely arbitrary *tour de force*. It is interesting in this regard to compare this interior with one almost exactly contemporary, the design for the Oak Room, in Miss Cranston's Ingram Street Tea-Rooms. While the similarity in the detailing is quite obvious, the Oak Room, being merely the refurbishing of an existing interior, with neither the structural problem nor the opportunities of the library, has in turn none of its spatial interest.

It would seem that in the structuring of a space out of timber, all Mackintosh's various skills and preoccupations could happily run together – the interest in problems of structural assembly, his

experience as a designer of furniture, his fascination
with line and surface, and his happy fusion of tradition and inventiveness. The traditions he acknow-
ledges in the library interior are clear, but the
acknowledgement is anything but servile. To use
his own words, he would not be guilty of 'feebly
imitating some of the visible and superficial features
of beautiful old works and neglecting the spirit,
the intention, the soul that lies beneath'. Certainly
the spirit of many kinds of old works can be seen,
although the forms are never quite the same. The
whole approach to the beam-and-column framing
is reminiscent of the Japanese, and at the same time
perhaps of Gothic architecture, in the way the
columns pick up the loading of the gallery beams
by means of extra members, 'cluster piers', clamped
on the sides of the main columns. And there are odd
Arts and Crafts whimsicalities, such as patterns of
tiny protruding dowels at tenoned joints, and the
graphic use of the old English device called the
'waggon chamfer' on the free balusters seen between
the columns and the solid gallery balustrade. The
'waggon chamfer', is the pattern of small successive
bites taken out of the edges of rectangular wooden
members, and belonged traditionally to the coach-
building and waggon-building crafts. It was introduced as a decorative device for furniture and architecture by the short-lived Kenton & Co., whose
moving spirits were Lethaby, Reginald Blomfield,
Sydney and Ernest Barnsley, and Ernest Gimson.
The device, and variations on it, became subsequently almost a hallmark of the Cotswold work of
Gimson and the brothers Barnsley, and it is probably
no coincidence to see it emerging in Mackintosh's
vocabulary.

But in spite of the presence of such elements, the
all-too-quaint nostalgia of the Arts and Crafts
mentality, which had been evident in his handling
of the timber framing of the Art School main
stair and museum, had now quite disappeared.

96, 97 Glasgow School of Art. Wrought iron
'knots' to tee-beams, and *opposite,* one of the
studios with easels designed by Mackintosh.

There is a crispness, an incisiveness, which we recognise as being wholly modern in feeling, even though it is emphatically not revolutionary in intent.

It is on the west façade, generated by and expressive of this library interior, that the modern feeling reaches perhaps its highest pitch. Yet here again it is a question of feeling, of the architect's individual handling of the forms, rather than of the origin of the forms themselves or their material. Characteristically, the disposition of the windows and their sizes is a direct reflection of the plan. And their grouping into continuous vertical bays is a grammatical device initiated by Norman Shaw, picked up by Voysey, Lethaby, and any number of late Victorians – and, of course, used by Mackintosh himself ten years before at the main entrance to this self-same building, with the linking of the ground-floor office and the Director's room. This particular relationship is rather important to an understanding of much of Mackintosh's formal handling, for he undoubtedly used such devices as these as 'motifs', in a compositional approach analogous to music. In his lecture on 'Seemliness' he had said: 'What one misses in . . . most . . . work . . . is – the large rhythm that undulates through that of the great masters ancient and modern – the sustained note of informing purpose – the deep vibration of some unifying undertone now rising to accent and emphasis – now sounding faintly, beneath the multifariousness of accompanying motives – but always visible to an attentive sense as the basis if not the burden of the theme with variations – the ensemble which every artist's work – no matter how trivial, should constitute.'

Taken in this way, it can be seen how the form of the bay window at the main entrance, and its faint echo in the engaged octagonal tower on the east face, was picked up as a linking theme and a point of departure for the treatment of the new wing. It is the dominant form on the west façade, and then around the corner on the south it is repeated, this

98 *Opposite*. Light pendant and decorated pilasters in the Board Room.
99 Window seats in the west corridor leading to the Library.

102 Glasgow School of Art.
The Library from gallery level.

time inset flush with the face of the wall. It then recurs, squatter and fatter, as three seating alcoves on the south face of the top-floor loggia. 99

But having acknowledged the provenance of the bays, it is still startlingly apparent that there is a great change in the manner of their use, the difference that is apparent between the handling of the east and west elevations of the building. This is, of course, a measure of Mackintosh's development over the intervening decade, a similar contrast as between the Martyrs' Public School and the Scotland Street 18 School. But it is also a measure of the change in Bri- 86 tish architecture generally, and the west façade can be related as directly to some contemporary building as could the east. Summerson has pointed out the similarity in treatment between the west wing and Charles Holden's design for the Central Reference Library in Bristol, drawings of which were 105 published in *The Builder* for September 2nd, 1895, and which would, almost certainly be known to Mackintosh. There is also, for what it is worth, a remote kind of ideological link-up between the work of the two men. Mackintosh was confessedly an admirer of J. D. Sedding, and elements of Sedding and of his pupil Henry Wilson are apparent in much of Mackintosh's work, particularly the ecclesiastical designs. Holden in his turn admitted to being at this period chiefly indebted in his work to Henry Wilson. In others of Holden's designs of this period, too, there can be seen the same rigid, attenuated rectangularity although without perhaps the drama of Mackintosh's work, notably the British Medical Association building in the Strand, London, and in 106 the extension to the Law Society headquarters in Chancery Lane.

Summerson has also drawn attention to the 'acute experience – direct or indirect – of Michelangelo' in Mackintosh's library wing, and evident in much of the English work of the period. There is reason to believe that this very evident interest in and sym-

103 Glasgow School of Art. Section through
the Library and Lecture Room.
104 *Opposite*. Studio above the Library.

SECTION D.D.

pathy with the drama and distortion of Michelangelo's architecture was related to the general interest in the 'transitional' styles of architecture referred to earlier. Many architects, including Mackintosh, were much more interested in the possibility of manipulation and synthesis of historical elements than in the analysis and faithful reproduction of entire historical vocabularies. Certainly the interest in Michelangelo was marked at this time. Beresford Pite, with whose work Mackintosh was familiar – notably the Institute of Chartered Accountants building produced under John Belcher's name – wrote a long and detailed study on Michelangelo's architecture in the *Architectural Review* during 1898, and Pite's successor as Belcher's 'ghost', John James Joass produced in London the Royal Insurance Company building in 1907 with as clear an indebtedness to Michelangelo as any English building has had.

Joass had been trained in Glasgow under John Burnet, and was probably a personal acquaintance of Mackintosh's. At any rate, there is a notable kinship which might have been more evident had the prepared cylinders in Mackintosh's library windows ever received their intended figure sculpture.

There is a pencilled note on Mackintosh's contract drawings which seems to indicate his intention that three of these figure carvings were to be of Cellini, St Francis, and Palladio. An ill-assorted trio, and yet curiously apposite, for Mackintosh's central architectural achievement may well be regarded as the dramatic reconciliation of strange bed-fellows. This certainly is what the completed Art School represents; it is an incredible and effective fusion of a whole series of different and disparate streams evident on the British scene in the last decade of the 19th century and the first of this. There is no element in the building which cannot be related, directly or indirectly, to contemporary British work, and the fact that many of the sources for his inspira-

NEW CENTRAL REFERENCE
LIBRARY ᵇ FOR THE CITY ⅋
COUNTY OF BRISTOL ᵉ FRONT
TO THE DEANERY ROAD ☺.
H PERCY ADAMS, F R I B A
Architect

tion regarded themselves as mutually exclusive can be forgotten in the entity of this building.

Yet there is no evidence that Mackintosh was trying – in 20th-century terms – to be modern. He was certainly not trying to create a new technological image; exposed steel, plate glass, and concrete were not considered remarkable enough for special comment at the time, being simply the expression of the particular economy of the building, and the entire emphasis is on those hand-wrought elements made from traditional materials. Nor was he overtly expressing a new attitude to space – although his handling of space was superb – for in the only part of this building where the spatial emphasis is unusual, it grew from a particular structural context. Nor was he preoccupied with structural virtuosity for its own sake, although he exploited structure as a springboard for decorative fantasy. For some curious reason, the small flower-conservatory projecting from the upper south-face of the library wing has suggested to some a great structural daring. But this is not the clear cantilever that it appears to be from some points of view, lying as it does in the re-entrant angle between the studio wall and the stair wall; it has a respectable ancestry in a hundred Scottish and French castle walls, and it lies, after all, only a cannon shot from the Clyde, beside whose everyday engineering practice it paled, even then, into insignificance.

Nevertheless, the Art School represents an earnest attempt to be 'modern' – not in 20th-century terms, but in 19th. Its emphasis was not on technology, space, and structure, but on function, method, and iconography.

140

105 *Opposite*. H. Percy Adams
(Designer: Charles Holden). Central
Reference Library, Bristol. 1895.
106 Charles Holden. The British Medical
Association Headquarters in The Strand,
London.

CHAPTER EIGHT 1909-1928

The Art School was completed in 1909. During the three years involved in the design and construction of the second phase, Mackintosh had designed several tea-rooms for Miss Cranston, continued work on her residence 'Hous 'hill', and designed at least two other houses, 'Mosside', Kilmacolm, and 'Auchinibert', Killearn, in neither of which had he been blessed with the degree of client support provided in the earlier house projects, and in neither of which had the vision and promise of the earlier houses been retained.

It seemed clear from the few drawings which survive that 'Mosside' was not built as originally designed, and it has undergone subsequent alteration and expansion. But although the fabric as it now stands is of little interest, the drawings remaining are the most forcible evidence of Mackintosh's preoccupation with the Scottish vernacular. They could well be one of Robert Lorimer's more modest productions. In the case of 'Auchinibert', it is said that during the construction Mackintosh was already displaying his search for release in alcohol, and his supervision was less than responsible. In the end, the completion of the work was entrusted to another architect.

It would be irresponsible to try to explain why this man, at the height of his developed powers and opportunities, should have turned to drink. It did not accord with his personal and visual fastidiousness, in whose home the teas were 'not lavish, but exquisite' – but it is a common enough incongruity. And there were clear reasons for strain.

Perhaps the first, and the one which is most speculative, was his own personality. The picture of the man that emerges from the all too little evidence is of a tense and hypersensitive person – certainly of a man of forcible opinions and high idealism, capable of immense expenditure of energy and of intense depression, warm-hearted and yet sensitive to criticism. He could respond with enthusiasm to support and approbation, and perhaps even to outright personal opposition, but he was more and more being hamstrung by the obduracy of local officialdom and by the lack of understanding and support of his peers.

Added to this, his manner of working was not designed to endear him to either his clients or his partner. In the pursuit of perfection, the changes, the voluminous detailing, the demands on time and skill from building operatives, took account of neither his clients' nor his own firm's patience or purse. Others who had used this particular approach to building design had experienced similar difficulty. Philip Webb, the archetype, had never undertaken more than a single job at a time, and his income throughout a notable and immensly influential career had never been more than barely sufficient for his own modest needs. Lethaby, again highly respected and influential, effectively retired from active building from 1904, at the age of 47, due to the nervous strain imposed by it. And Mackintosh, whose collective output during these years was considerable, and whose authoritarian approach did not ease the demands, must have suffered stresses that can only be guessed at. A joiner who had worked under his direction on furniture commissions recalled wryly after half a century: 'There was nae palaver wi' Charlie.' He would brook no opposition in the pursuit of his objectives.

In all this he had, of course, the unabated support of his Continental admirers. But, flattering as it must have been, it was not the support he most needed. What he needed above all was the support of those at home who could both provide more amenable working opportunities, and who could understand and share a common architectural heritage. There is no evidence that his Continental emulators appreciated anything in his architectural work beyond its graphic and decorative mannerism and the more self-evident aspects of its functionalism.

XII Watercolour scheme for
wall decoration at 78,
Derngate, Northampton. 1915.
Royal Institute of British
Architects Drawings
Collection.

XIII *Fort Maillert*, 1927.
Watercolour in the University
of Glasgow. Mackintosh
Collection.

107 The living room at 78, Derngate,
Northampton. 1915–16

Thus as Mackintosh reached an effective architectural maturity, he almost concurrently found himself in an isolation which was becoming unbearable. And over the four years from the completion of the Art School in 1909 to 1913, his architectural output was marginal.

During 1910 and 1911 Mackintosh was engaged on the last two interiors at Miss Cranston's Ingram Street Tea-Rooms, the Cloister Room and the China Tea-Room. These are of interest in that they show more markedly a stylistic development that was emerging in his last work at the Art School. This was the preoccupation with severely rectilinear forms, not just for the constructive framework for his buildings and furniture, but for the decorative patterns as well. The long, complex curves of his early graphic manner were virtually gone, and were being replaced by a much more staccato ornamentation rather like the 'waggon-chamfering' in the library interior, and the parallel zig-zags seen on the architrave of the west entrance. These two motifs, indeed, form almost the entire basis for the decoration of the Cloister Room, and they produce a character markedly different from any of the earlier interiors and certainly not as clearly resolved. The China Tea-Room is also strongly rectilinear, this time composed of repetitive squares in the form of latticed screens and wall panels, a form which had been evident in his architectural and decorative work from the beginning, although never so obsessive.

The demise of the long curves and the implicit animal-vegetable symbolism concurs more or less with the rapid disappearance of Art Nouveau ornament throughout Europe, but it is not likely that Mackintosh's abandonment of these forms can be attributed simply to a superficial change in taste. His own stated intentions were too serious to be diverted by such a change.

The growing dependence on straight lines did not indicate a waning interest in ornament itself. Indeed,

these two interiors have less simple serenity than almost any of his earlier work.

During the time that these works were being carried out, Mackintosh's personal affairs were rapidly deteriorating. The working routine at the office was becoming less and less bearable, and he was succeeding in antagonising clients and colleagues alike. Keppie, who had become before this President of the Glasgow Institute of Architects, and was a leading professional figure in the city, had nothing in common architecturally with his wilful, brilliant partner, and had shown, all in all, remarkable tolerance in their relationship. But now both partners clearly required an escape from one another. The end came in 1913 when Mackintosh resigned, ostensibly in protest over an office submission to a local competition.

The following year the Mackintoshes closed their Glasgow home and moved to the village of Walberswick on the Suffolk coast, where there was a small artists' colony frequented by the Newberys. While there, resting, painting, and debating the uncertain future, war was declared and one possibility for Mackintosh's future was firmly eliminated. He had been invited to join his Continental friends, and was in correspondence with the Austrian secessionists. Whether he ever seriously contemplated a permanent move of this kind is impossible to say, but the war in any event precluded it,

In 1915 the Mackintoshes moved to London and, inevitably, took rooms in Chelsea. But war had brought building to a standstill and they were without influential connections. Prospects were far from heartening. However, in the following year Mackintosh did obtain one small commission, and this from a potentially influential client. W. J. Bassett-Lowke was the proprietor of the well-known model-making firm of that name, and he commissioned Mackintosh to alter and redecorate a small terrace-house in Northampton, No. 78 Derngate.

108 Proposed artist's studios for the Arts League of Service. Elevation to Glebe Place. (This drawing and figures 109 and 110 in the collection of Mr and Mrs H. Jefferson Barnes.)

THREE CHELSEA STUDIOS.
ELEVATION TO GLEBE PLACE.

The interiors of the completed house are a startling departure from the Glasgow work, although they can be seen to link with the Cloister Room and the China Tea-Room in certain details. All hint of modelling and of the tense linear quality of his early work has disappeared, and been replaced by staccato, hard-edged patterns which almost uncannily forecast decorative preoccupations of the next two decades. Here for the first time can be seen a direct indebtedness to Austrian work – Howarth has pointed out the source of the triangular patterning in the work of Josef Urban of Vienna, illustrated in *The Studio* special number on 'The Art Revival in Austria' published in 1906. But the indebtedness is not entirely Continental, for in the furniture particularly can be seen a clear relationship with such work as the later Gimson designs, and particularly Ambrose Heal's London furniture.

The narrow elevation to the garden was completely altered by Mackintosh, as a result of the

XII
107

109 Chelsea Studios. Elevation to
Cheyne House Garden.

provision of a small extension. Here the indebtedness to the Viennese is complete, and it could quite easily have been a product of Josef Hoffman or Adolf Loos. There is none of the particular Scottish character of Mackintosh's earlier work – which is hardly surprising in a terrace-house in Northampton, nor is there any dependence on vernacular detailing. It is, of course, far too small a thing on which to base any judgment, but it does seem to represent the effort of the man to shake off the last vestiges of the past he had so irrevocably left behind him.

During the following years in Chelsea, the Mackintoshes occupied the bulk of their time with fabric designs, water-colours, some small decorative commissions from Miss Cranston and other Glasgow friends, and various communal activities within the Chelsea artistic colony, including some theatrical design for 'The Plough' a short-lived but successful dramatic group. They were interesting but marginal activities, and they must have done little to restore Mackintosh's shaken equilibrium.

In 1920, however, a genuine architectural opportunity arrived. In rapid succession Mackintosh was requested by three artist friends in the Chelsea community to design houses and studios, two of them on adjacent sites. Shortly thereafter Mackintosh was commissioned to design a block of studio flats for the Arts League of Service for a site adjoining two of the artists' premises, those of Derwent Wood and Harold Squire.

Although Squire and Wood were involved with the Arts League of Service, the three premises being on adjoining sites and design work on each proceeding concurrently, there is a curious absence of affinity between the various building elements in the group designs that emerged. The complexity of forms and the restlessness of the broken surfaces can be traced in part to the planning, for there is evidently the same determination to generate the building forms by the plan, but this is not a complete explanation. And there are evident traditional elements and materials, this time naturally enough the domestic traditions of old Chelsea rather than those of Scotland, mixed with Mackintosh's later decorative manner. There is also more than a passing affinity with C. R. Ashbee's houses in neighbouring Cheyne Walk, with which Mackintosh was familiar.

But the scheme never came to fruition, although permission to build was eventually and reluctantly given by the Ecclesiastical Commissioners. The designs as they stand must be regarded, in the typical Mackintosh manner, as merely intentional, and what they might have become with his inventive and detailed shaping through the building process cannot be known. Whether, indeed, Mackintosh was any longer capable of the sustained driving effort required to carry out this process is questionable, although he did execute a smaller and quite different scheme for Harold Squire on the intended site. No precise description of the finished building is obtainable, but it does not appear to have been of major architectural interest, and Squire did not occupy it for long.

In the same year, 1920, Mackintosh was commissioned by Margaret Morris to design a theatre. His design was objected to strongly by the authorities, and without providing an alternative scheme, the project was eventually abandoned. The drawings indicate a formal, symmetrical disposition, with a relatively unadorned monumentality closely akin to the work of the Viennese secessionists, not so much in detail as in feeling and intent. His current preoccupation with linear repetition and stepped surfaces can be seen in the immense and cavernous architrave around the main entrance, a form which can be related to, although only marginally justified by, the internal staircases. By and large, it is an assemblage of symmetrical forms which do not bear close functional inspection, a composition which

108
109
110

110 Proposed block of studios for the Arts
League of Service. Plan and elevation.

FRONT ELEVATION.   SECTION ON A:B.   SECTION ON C:D.

relies far more on its image of 'modernity' and less on its generation by use than his mature Glasgow work.

Except for one or two small cottage designs during this period, Mackintosh's architectural work was finished. The one definite impression of these works subsequent to his departure from Glasgow, is of a man who has lost his way. His great abilities could still be seen from time to time, and even the possibility of new and fascinating departures – particularly as seen in the Northampton interiors. But the image is cloudy, the intent is uncertain.

The departure from Scotland was traumatic in its effect on his work, apart from his personal decline, for the central core and pivot of his design effort had been its Scottish indigenous dependence. And no matter how far his inventive capacities led him, he was never quite out of touch with native materials, methods, and forms. In the south, he was too old, too disenchanted, and too dispirited to begin this process again, and the tide of taste and popular opinion was running too strongly in another direction to tolerate the 'foreign' experiments of a middle-aged rebel. His only allies were those who, in the end, could not afford to build.

In 1923 the Mackintoshes left Chelsea and settled in Port Vendres on the Mediterranean coast of southern France. Here, for four years, Charles devoted himself entirely to water-colour painting. The change of scene and the new pursuit had apparently been largely at Margaret's instigation, who had borne patiently and devotedly the years of trial and disappointment. To a considerable extent the change worked well. His drinking became more moderate, and in the challenge of a new, but not unfamiliar, discipline he was able to begin to work again. For four years the couple lived quietly, and apparently happily, at Port Vendres, and the product of this time was a collection of some forty water-colour paintings of considerable quality, and great interest. Mackintosh had of course painted and sketched throughout his career, but exquisite as much of this work had been, it was largely concerned with the recording of buildings, scenes, and vegetation – as a corollary and aid to his primary architectural activity. These paintings in France represent an entirely different departure; they are the work of a man who was now attempting to channel his entire expression through this medium.

The paintings fall into two groups; still-life studies of plants and flower groups, and landscapes. The flower studies are the culmination of a type of drawing and painting he had always been doing, spare, linear works of a pronouncedly Japanese quality, superbly botanical in their accuracy, and yet clear and elegant in their economy.

The landscapes, however, are the works that betray the new purpose in his painting. They have, of course, a clear provenance in the architectural sketches he had been producing since his youth, and indeed, a painting of 1927 entitled *Le Fort Maillert* bears a remarkable resemblance to some of his sketches at Holy Island in 1902. But clearly his concern was no longer simply to record nature, or even some aspect of the natural scene, but to manipulate and shape the seen objects to his own purposes. The inevitable irony of these paintings is that they are, above all things, architectural. Not only are they architectural in the deliberate and precise way that the elements are composed and built up, but the very forms and linear patterns betray a startling relationship with his later architectural designs. His 1927 study *The Rocks*, for instance, can be directly compared with the detailing of the fireplace surround in the Bassett-Lowke interior, or indeed with the entrance architrave for Margaret Morris's theatre. And throughout these works is seen his life-long preoccupation with line and surface. Virtually devoid of modelling and of any atmospheric effects, whatever spatial effects they achieve are obtained through the implicit relationships of plane and line. The colours, too, are no longer the pale monochromatic arrangements with subtle accents, but rich, full, and vital.

Seen in the context of his life's work, these paintings are the tangible evidence of an unrealised potential. They have all the graphic control and certainty that made the Art School what it is. They have taken the idiom of his latest, and uncertain, architectural works and demonstrated that this manner, too, could be related directly to his touchstone, Nature. In a curious and poignant sense these paintings could have been built.

But this was no longer possible. In the autumn of 1927 Mackintosh complained of a sore throat and on medical advice returned with Margaret to London for specialist examination. Cancer of the tongue and throat was diagnosed, and he underwent radium treatment. He made a brief recovery and was released from hospital. But after some months he was admitted to a nursing home, where, on December 10th, 1928, he died. Margaret Mackintosh did not survive her husband long. Four years later, on January 10th, 1933, she died after a brief illness, in Chelsea.

In the University of Glasgow files, there is a small collection of letters relating to the disposition of the effects of the two studios after Margaret's death. Among the sad and concerned letters of a few friends is a terse and indifferent letter with an accompanying schedule from a firm of London valuers, listing the contents of the Chelsea studios. Furniture, personal effects, a large collection of sketches and architectural drawings, and thirty-one paintings were stated to be 'practically of no value', and the sum of £88 16s 2d was put on the total. Contributing to this total was a nominal value of £1 on four chairs of his own design. It would be unwise to moralise on the strength of market prices, but the letter and schedule seem an entirely consistent conclusion to the apathy of an era.

CHAPTER NINE RETROSPECT

It is important to realise that the work by which Mackintosh's reputation has been established was the product of little more than a single decade, begun by, and finishing with, the Glasgow School of Art. He sprang into being, almost fully formed, in 1896, and faded almost as quickly after 1906. His rise to prominence is entirely comprehensible in his ability, energy, and not more than the usual amount of good fortune. The reasons for his rapid decline are not nearly so simple.

Certainly his architectural isolation within his own generation must have been a major contributor to his disintegration. To understand this isolation, and in turn to understand the measure of his own contribution to the architectural picture of the times, some attempt must be made to delineate the major cross-currents of taste and ideals that prevailed during his working lifetime.

Underlying the theoretical developments outlined in the first chapter was a broad stream of rampant, undisciplined eclecticism, stimulated, particularly from 1870 onwards, by those serious theoreticians who were attempting to bring new relevance to their art by the principle of 'development' or 'absorption', but as practised by the ordinary and unconcerned practitioners, pastiches of the most extraordinary borrowings. It was an attitude of incredibly bemused optimism, captured precisely by A. E. Street, the not very distinguished son of the very distinguished Gothic Revivalist, G. E. Street, in an *Architectural Review* article of 1901 on 'Architecture in the Victorian Era': 'The Purist of an earlier day would be shocked at the freedom and individuality with which the raw material of style is handled now, while the stickler for an ethical basis in architecture would hold his hands aloft to see the cheerful eclecticism with which the designer today skips from century to century, or stands with feet wide apart while the ages roll between. . . . If an elasticity of appreciativeness which will stretch to

include examples of every style is to be aimed at, then we are near our mark.'

This was hardly a state of affairs that would satisfy those seriously concerned with producing a coherent, recognisable architectural style for their time. And, from about 1894, a movement with just this intent was quickly gaining momentum. It was spearheaded by that ageing, but still versatile master of image-making, Norman Shaw, and abetted by such younger devotees as Reginald Blomfield. With such designs as Chesters, Northumberland (1892), and Bryanston, Dorset (1890), Shaw heralded the return to the comparative order and respectability of the English Renaissance, and the younger men were quick to seize on its benefits. Here was the opportunity to realign architecture with academic taste and scholarship, to re-establish canons of proportion and of composition, and withal to pay lip service to the ideas of native tradition and indigenous development which had characterised the previous decades.

It was no coincidence that, concurrently with the rise of this neo-Renaissance movement, architectural education was finally becoming established in Britain as an academic discipline, and the profession itself was, through the medium of the Royal Institute of British Architects, slowly succeeding in defining for itself a legal, and a social, status. In the architecture of the English Renaissance could be found the basis for teaching, assessment, and examination – in short, for regularised instruction in that most subjective of disciplines, design. Similarly, on the professional level, it provided an imagery which could be instantly recognised by society at large, and one which coincided with the notably self-conscious jingoism of the time.

This peculiar brand of national self-awareness was, at least in architecture, stimulated in part by the penetration of Britain's insularity. There was a growing awareness of the international prestige of the French Beaux Arts training, of the disciplined achievements of Germany, and even of the very substantial developments, technical and otherwise, of the upstart American cousins. In the case of the latter, there is almost an element of resentment that they were no longer dependent on the James Gibbs pattern books.

In all this, there was very little room for the William Morris social ideal of the band of happy craftsmen, all social distinctions gone, working together for the common weal. And there was little room either for the kind of abstract symbolism that had emerged out of the brief Art Nouveau exercises. Although Lethaby had, more than any other, fashioned a meaningful approach out of the Morris doctrine, it was foredoomed to failure under the weight of the prevailing ethos.

It was with those architects who, although not forming in any sense a cohesive school, linked most closely with the Morris and Lethaby ideology, that Mackintosh's early sympathy and admiration lay. His isolation from them, on the grounds of a quite misleading imagery, was an immeasurable loss to the architecture of the time.

Both Lethaby and Mackintosh, as has been seen, wrestled with the problem of an architectural iconography for the time. Mackintosh's solution was the natural outcome of his graphic interests, and, although he did not remain bound to the swirling lines and mystical symbolism of his early work, the attempt to 'decorate' in a way which related to both function and Nature can be seen to permeate his work unabated throughout his life.

Lethaby, on the other hand, although he abandoned the practice of architecture, had concluded relatively early, certainly before 1911, that the relevance of ornament had passed. He expressed this in the rewritten version of *Architecture, Mysticism and Myth* which was published serially in *The Builder* in 1928 as *Architecture, Nature and Magic*: 'Ornamentation in its origins and growth was to protect and promote well-being. Now that the magic has gone out of it, unless some new content of nature and meaning is restored, it will die. Much is already dead, as we are slowly realising, and it will pass more and more out of the building customs of the future'.

To a profession carefully building its public image and preening itself above all else on its artistic role in society, this was very cold fare indeed. And certainly Lethaby's proposal would have necessitated a professional revolution, and a revolution in training, as great as the social revolution required by Morris a generation earlier. No one, in any event, was interested in the idea of an architecture without 'style'. The functionalist stream, therefore, tended to revert to a kind of Arts and Crafts infancy, quite out of tune with the challenges and possibilities of the times, or to be absorbed into the neo-Renaissance revival that was developing. In its absorption into this stylistic constriction, it lost the freedom and functional flexibility that had so excitingly begun to emerge in the latter part of the 19th century.

This, of course, was where Mackintosh's contribution was so relevant, for he developed an architectural idiom which was firmly based on the British functional tradition, and yet which, by his graphic ability, was given a recognisable visual imagery. That this imagery, as it is seen in his early work, would be a fairly rapidly passing phase is evident by the way in which it had noticeably changed after 1904, and particularly in the very late works. But that does not destroy its importance. For what Mackintosh tangibly demonstrated was that a widely disparate set of threads, each of them in its way unique to the time, could be pulled together into a coherent architectural style; a style, moreover, that was capable of consistent and rapid development, and of all the functional flexibility, the capacity to absorb new functions and new materials, that had characterised the best of the earlier work.

The irony is that it was this very imagery, or at

least its first manifestation, which was the cause of Mackintosh's isolation from his natural English brethren. Although the nature of this opposition has already been discussed, it must be stressed that the objection of the Lethaby group centred essentially around the very attempt to introduce a new 'style', and not the specific imagery of the style itself. They felt, and with some justification, that the pursuit of such a goal could only lead to the seduction away from the prior considerations of function and technique. What Mackintosh proved was that there was at least one man who could achieve all three.

It is entirely possible that the kind of synthesis that Mackintosh achieved could only have occurred in the relative separation of a provincial city, where an intimate knowledge of the rivalries and cross-currents that motivated various groups was perhaps not directly realised. Whether this is true or not, it is certain that, having developed this personal idiom, it had less practical chance of exploitation in a provincial city than in an ideological hotbed such as London, where his work could become directly known to those who shaped opinions. For it seems fairly certain that had there been first-hand acquaintance with his work, there would have been immediate recognition of its motivation. One man who may, in fact, have recognised the intrinsic qualities of Mackintosh's work, and who certainly had at least some acquaintance with it, was Baillie Scott, who said in a lecture given on behalf of the Worshipful Company of Carpenters in 1908: 'Do not be too ready to scorn what is called the "New Art". It is true the greater part of it is sorry stuff; but you will still find, amongst much that is affected and bizarre, here and there the right note struck: here and there the new thing which is also a good thing. It must also never be forgotten that all the old work we admire so much was new once, and when it first appeared it must have been as startling

in its novelty as any of the products of the "New Art" of our day.' This, from a dyed-in-the-wool Arts and Crafts man was bordering on the heretical, and was certainly as enthusiastic a reception as could have been expected.

But, by and large, there was simply no interest in Mackintosh and his efforts. To the English architects, he was simply one of the Glasgow 'spook school', and, as one of the potpourri of novelties picked up by *The Studio*, not to be taken too seriously.

In spite of the early enthusiasm of many younger men, and the continued support of friends like the Newberys and Miss Cranston, there is no evidence to suggest that Mackintosh ever found any architectural 'soul-mates' on the Glasgow scene. After the departure for Liverpool of Herbert MacNair, who never practised architecture in his own right, Mackintosh's closest friend professionally appears to have been James Salmon Jr., the son and grandson of established Glasgow architects. And although in Salmon's work many of the characteristic forms of the Glasgow Art Nouveau decorative details can be seen, they never effectively moved beyond the kind of work Mackintosh produced for Queen Margaret's Medical College.

Mackintosh's isolation in relation to the Continent was similar. Certainly he was not known to them on any scale until after the turn of the century, and, as has been noted, his exposure to the Europeans was almost entirely by means of exhibitions and limited decorative ventures.

Thus the remarkable fact is that while his mature style drew from many sources, he never had the benefit of an architectural dialogue with like minds. Nor was he able to share with those who might have benefited his own developing ideas.

For it is entirely clear from his own work that his ideas did expand and develop rapidly during his most productive decade. At the outset he was much preoccupied with decorative symbolism, and it was this that led him so compulsively to the title and contents of Lethaby's book. But with the inception of the Art School project, this symbolic interest became closely interwoven, with, and sometimes obscured by, the decorative possibilities of function and building structure. The graphically symbolic predilection continued, of course, and was particularly emphasised in the tea-room projects, but even in these, the growing interest in the actual manipulation of the bones and sinews of the building structure can be seen. He was directly aware of these two constituent aspects himself. In the 1902 paper 'Seemliness' quoted in Chapter Six, he said: 'The power which the artist possesses of representing objects to himself explains the hallucinating character of his work . . . their tendency towards symbolism – but the creative imagination is far more important. The artist cannot attain to mastery in his art unless he is endowed in the highest degree with the faculty of invention.' And this inventive capacity had to be centred on an '. . . understanding of the absolute and true requirements of a building or object'.

This inventive faculty, as manifested in the first wing of the Art School, was characterised by the shaping of forms, the subtle modelling of timber, masonry, and metal, that betrays craft-oriented, rather than technology-oriented thinking. This had nothing to do with relative plainness or embellishment, but with the actual forms of the pieces with which the assemblage was composed. Over the following decade, Mackintosh moved consciously towards a decorative inventiveness which relied much more on the cumulative effect of the assembly of pieces than on the forms of the pieces themselves. A comparison between the woodwork of the Art School museum and the library interior makes this clear.

The few works that Mackintosh executed after leaving Glasgow show an unmistakable decline in his capacity, not surprisingly. But they do demonstrate the continued decorative tendency in this direction, and in the final, brief flowering of his talent in the water-colour paintings, a hint is shown of what this might have become in architectural terms.

One aspect of his times, however, with which Mackintosh never did come to terms, was the changed role of the architect in society. Although the profession had been established in more or less its present state by the time Mackintosh began, only during the last decades of the 19th century was it beginning to face the really demanding tasks of building for a growing variety of functions within strict limits of economy and performance. Problems of accounting (and accountability), of contract law, of specification and information were all constricting the artistic autonomy that the architect tended to feel – particularly if he read Ruskin – was his due. Within this more and more impersonal working framework, where every party to the building enterprise was constrained by documentation, it became a continuous battle for Mackintosh – and others of the same persuasion – to manipulate, refine, and improve their projects as they developed. And the multiple frictions resulting from his insistence on doing just this must not be underestimated; they may well have been one of the major factors contributing to his collapse.

What, then, was Mackintosh's influence on the architecture of his time? Effectively, none. His greatest admirers and constant supporters were the Austrian secessionists. But while, as Howarth has pointed out, there are marginal evidences of his early decorative influence in some of their interior and furniture designs, his architectural roots were far removed from theirs. In their eulogies of his design the emphasis is entirely on those decorative qualities which the historians of the modern movement in architecture have deplored. He had certainly none of the fundamental impact on Euro-

112 *La Rue du Soleil*. 1927. Watercolour in the University of Glasgow. Mackintosh Collection.

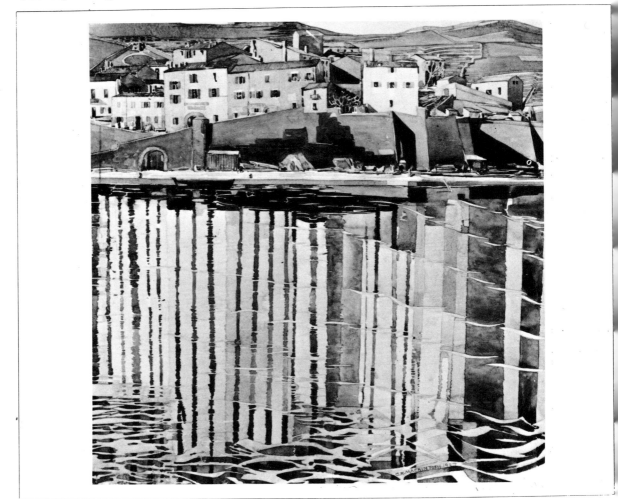

pean architecture that Frank Lloyd Wright, his contemporary, had through the Wasmuth publications of 1910.

In Britain, his architectural eclipse was total. He can scarcely, therefore, be considered a pioneer of modern architecture in the usual sense of having contributed to a developing collective ideology, or even to a developing vocabulary of form.

But he was not, therefore, a total phenomenon, an isolated genius without ancestry or progeny. He was rather a last and remote efflorescence of a vital British tradition which reached back to Pugin. He could not perhaps have existed apart from his isolation, but he could not in the end have any succession because of it. With his pursuit of the 'modern', his love of the old, and his obsessive individuality, he was one of the last and one of the greatest of the Victorians.

156

INDEX

ACKNOWLEDGMENTS

Photographs were provided by the following

COLOUR PLATES

Michael Holford Plates II, XII; Keith Gibson Plates I, III, IV, V, VI, VII, VIII, IX, X, XI, XIII.

BLACK AND WHITE ILLUSTRATIONS

T. & R. Annan & Sons half-title, 39, 40, 48, 73, 75, 76, 107; Mr. & Mrs. H. Jefferson Barnes 108, 109, 110; Keith Gibson frontispiece, 15, 19, 20, 21, 24, 26, 27, 28, 29, 31, 32, 33, 34, 35, 36, 37, 38, 42, 43, 44, 45, 46, 47, 52, 53, 60, 61, 62, 63, 64, 65, 66, 67, 71, 74, 77, 78, 79, 84, 85, 91, 92, 93, 94, 95, 96, 97, 98, 99, 100, 101, 102, 104, 112; Glasgow School of Art 22, 23; Michael Holford 30, 56, 57, 58, 59; A. F. Kersting 1, 2, 51; National Monuments Record 25; Royal Institute of British Architects 3, 4, 5, 8, 9, 10, 16, 17, 18, 86, 87, 105, 106; University of Glasgow: Mackintosh Collection 6, 7, 11, 12, 13, 14, 41, 49, 50, 55, 69, 70, 72, 80, 81, 82, 83, 88, 90, 103, 111.

ILLUSTRATIONS FROM CONTEMPORARY PUBLICATIONS ARE AS FOLLOWS:

The Architect June 10th, 1891; figs. 3, 4; *The Architect* July 10th, 1891: fig. 5; *The British Architect* February 24th, 1893: figs. 8, 9; *The Architect* June 20th, 1890: fig. 10; *The British Architect* January 10th, 1896: figs. 16, 17; *Academy Architecture* 1904: figs. 86, 87; *The Builder* September 2nd, 1905: fig. 105; *Academy Architecture II* 1908: fig. 106.

A copy of *Haus eines Kunstfreundes* published by Alexander Koch (Darmstadt 1902) was kindly lent by the Librarian of Glasgow School of Art from which Plate II and figures 56, 57, 58 and 59 are reproduced.